Clear Thinking
for Composition

Clear Thinking for Composition

FIFTH EDITION

RAY KYTLE
CENTRAL MICHIGAN UNIVERSITY

McGraw-Hill, Inc.
New York St. Louis San Francisco Auckland Bogotá
Caracas Lisbon London Madrid Mexico City Milan
Montreal New Delhi San Juan Singapore
Sydney Tokyo Toronto

This book is printed on acid-free paper.

Fifth Edition

90 DOC/DOC 9987

CLEAR THINKING FOR COMPOSITION

Library of Congress Cataloging-in-Publication Data

Kytle, Ray.
    Clear Thinking for composition.

    Bibliography: p.
    Includes index.
    1. English language—Rhetoric.   2. Logic   I. Title
PE1408.K9 1986   808'.042   86–6710
ISBN 0-07-553969-1

For Dennis and Carol Farley

PREFACE

Clear Thinking for Composition is designed to communicate to the student the reasoning skills essential to convincing and responsible writing. In the course of pursuing this goal, the text should also facilitate a deeper understanding of the roots of illogic. For clear thinking is not simply a matter of recognizing and avoiding fallacies. We must also be aware of the power and pervasiveness of other forces—cultural, psychological, linguistic—that militate against sound reasoning in our own discourse and encourage acquiesence in the unsound reasoning of others.

ORGANIZATION

Overall, the organization of the text is sequential and incremental. Section One introduces analysis as both a method of logical inquiry and a heuristic technique. Section Two discusses the manner in which our cultural assumptions, our psychological makeup, and our linguistic heritage severally and collectively promote faulty reasoning. Section Three, the "logic core" of the text, explains in depth and breadth the specific reasoning errors to which inductive and deductive arguments are prone as well as the major fallacies of relevance that weaken any argument, whatever its form. In the context of this background, Section Four offers the student a unique acronym-based technique for exploring and discrediting faulty argument, whether it is manifested in the speech of others or in their writing. Finally, Section Five discusses the transition from clear thinking to effective writing—from reasoning to rhetoric.

Within this broad structure, however, a nonlinear approach is adopted. One of the reiterated premises of the text is that reasoning errors occur in, and are the product of, a total context. Hence, important concepts are alluded to and elaborated on at various points in the text whenever new material being discussed sheds additional light on them.

CHANGES IN THE FIFTH EDITION

In this edition, the most thoroughly revised since the book's inception, I have tried to exploit the paradox "more is less." To this end, all material that would normally be covered in a core composition text has been excised, allowing the discussion of critical thinking to be significantly expanded without a corollary increase in the length of the text.

Also new to this edition are the highlights that encapsulate key concepts from each chapter, the acronym-based "illogic detector" detailed in Section Four, student and professional essays that exemplify many of the concepts discussed, and the final section, "Reasoning and Rhetoric," which is intended to facilitate the transition from clear thinking to composition.

CONTENTS

THE PROCESS OF LOGICAL THINKING

Introduction

Logical thinking is a *process*. The process is relatively simple, it always works, and it can be readily mastered. In the process of logical thinking:

1. *Objectivity* is the prerequisite.
2. *Insight* is the goal.
3. *Analysis* is the method.

OBJECTIVITY

You have not mastered the process of logical thinking until you can achieve an open mind and an *objective attitude* toward any subject. In the dialogues that illustrate analysis and in Section Two, we will examine those forces and reasoning habits that insidiously undermine objectivity.

INSIGHT

Once you are able to achieve and maintain an open mind when analyzing a subject, you will not feel compelled to defend your preconceptions about it. Instead, your attitude will be: "I want to *understand* as much as possible about the subject. And I won't know what I'm going to say about the subject until I have gained as much *insight* as possible into it."

ANALYSIS

The way to achieve this insight is through *analysis*. You should not decide what you are going to say about the subject until *after* you have *analyzed* it.

Analysis is what this book is all about: how you do it, forces that interfere with it, fallacies that subvert it, subjects that require you to inform yourself prior to it. But before we set out, we should have firmly in mind the three principles that govern analysis. These principles are:

1. Examine the subject from various points of view.
2. Classify these points of view.
3. Recognize the complexity of the subject.

The importance of each of these three steps cannot be overemphasized. Looking at the subject from various points of view will lead you to *insight;* classifying these points of view will give *order and structure* to your essay; and recognizing the complexity of the subject will help you *avoid oversimplification.*

When you look at a given subject from as many points of view as possible, you will probably realize that the matter is more complex than you may have thought at first. And in many cases the subject will turn out to be so complex that you will have to acknowledge that no *general* law or principle concerning it can be laid down. This is especially true of broad subjects that, when analyzed, turn out to be composed of almost infinite variables. When you encounter such subjects, you must beware of making any categorical assertions about them. (A categorical assertion is an assertion without any qualification or condition: "Love is good"; "Honesty is the best policy.") Here are some examples of this type of subject:

Morality	Beauty
Détente	Liberty
Honor	Success

The point is that no single unqualified assertion about any of these subjects can possibly be valid because the subjects denote too many variables. Instead of making a categorical assertion about the subject, you must content yourself with an analysis of it (or of some aspect of it). To illustrate:

SUBJECT: LOVE

Point of View	Classification
1. What kind of love?	Type of love
2. Love of whom?	Object of love
3. Love for what purpose?	Motive of love

LIMITED SUBJECT: OBJECT OF LOVE

Point of View	Classification
1. Love of mother for child	Maternal love
2. Love of father for child	Paternal love
3. Love of child for parent	Filial love
4. Love of brother for sister	Brotherly love
5. Love of sister for brother	Sisterly love
6. Love of one's country	Patriotic love
7. Love for humankind	Humanitarian love
8. Love for the ill and weak	Compassionate love
9. Love for God	Religious love
10. Love for oneself	Narcissistic love
11. Love of another's body	Physical love

At this point we realize that when we classify love by the *object* of love, we come up with a *type* of love. For example, love of mother for child (object) is classified as maternal love (type). But each type of love can be further subdivided according to the *motives* or *needs* of the person loving. For instance, we may speak of *exploitative* maternal love, *supportive* maternal love, *possessive* maternal love, *nurturing* maternal love, *selfish* maternal love, *self-sacrificing* maternal love, and so forth. So, as is obvious, no generalization about "Love," no statement that "Love is . . . ," can possibly be accurate because any such categorical assertion *ignores the complexity of the subject.*

You may sometime find yourself with a subject that is simply too complex to work with. The tip-off is that, when you begin to analyze it, it just keeps on breaking down into smaller and smaller pieces, like a clod of dry earth. The more you handle it, the more it crumbles. In this case, you should work with one of the little pieces that crumbles off, not with the whole subject. For example, we found that maternal love broke down, when examined from different points of view, into such types as "exploitative," "possessive," and so forth. Take *one* of these subdivisions of a subdivision and work with it:

LIMITED SUBJECT: POSSESSIVE MATERNAL LOVE

Point of View	Classification
1. What are the characteristics of possessive maternal love?	Characteristics

2. What causes a mother to love
   in this way?   Causes
3. What are the effects of this
   type of love on the children?   Effects

SUMMARY

The process of logical thinking requires that you approach your subject with an open mind—with objectivity. The goals of logical thinking are insight and understanding. The method by which to achieve this insight is analysis. To analyze a subject, you look at it from as many points of view as possible and then classify these various points of view. You must always recognize and respect the complexity of the subject because failure to recognize its complexity will lead to oversimplification and, hence, to inaccuracy.

With these general remarks in mind, let us turn to some dialogues that show the process of analysis in action.

Analysis In Action

YVONNE AND THE RUNAWAY MOMS
A TALE OF RAGE AND REASON

Yvonne is a first-year college student of eighteen who was raised according to the gospel as pronounced by Marabel Morgan. Among other lessons, her parents taught her that no man likes a woman with brains, that tears make a woman appealing, and that motherhood is a woman's sacred duty.

When Yvonne left home for college, her worried parents warned her to watch out for radical young college instructors who would try to put wrong ideas in her head. Yvonne really didn't pay much attention, though she dutifully promised to watch out. But then, the very first day she walked into her English composition class, there was the young instructor she had been warned about. And sure enough, after the instructor checked the roll, she assigned an essay on, of all things, the subject "runaway mothers"! As soon as the other students had begun writing, Yvonne rushed to the front of the classroom, and the thrilling dialogue that follows began:

YVONNE (*incredulously*): By "runaway mothers" do you mean a mother who just up and leaves her husband and children?

INSTRUCTOR: Yes.

YVONNE (*impulsively*): Oh! That's terrible! Everybody knows that.

INSTRUCTOR: What do you mean, "terrible"?

YVONNE (*with conviction*): Wrong.

INSTRUCTOR: What do you mean, "wrong"?

YVONNE: She shouldn't do it.

INSTRUCTOR: Why not?

7

YVONNE (*becoming exasperated*): I already told you. Because it's *wrong!* How on earth can you ask me to write a whole theme about a subject like that? Running off and leaving your kids is wrong! Period. There's nothing more to say.

INSTRUCTOR: Do you see any advantages or good points about being a social worker?

YVONNE (*suspiciously*): What's that got to do with anything?

INSTRUCTOR: Do you?

YVONNE: Of course. There're lots of good points. Help people, do your part, all sorts of things.

INSTRUCTOR: Do you want to be a social worker?

YVONNE: Ugh! Icky people!

INSTRUCTOR: Social workers?

YVONNE: No, of course not. The people social workers work with.

INSTRUCTOR: Well then?

YVONNE: Well then, what? You're trying to trap me.

INSTRUCTOR: Well then, you can see reasons why a person might choose to be a social worker, but you don't feel that recognizing them means you have to become one.

YVONNE: Of course not.

INSTRUCTOR: Then why not approach the subject of runaway mothers the same way? That is, try to discover some reasons why a mother might decide to leave her husband and children.

YVONNE (*disgustedly*): I just don't understand you. Walking out on your husband and children is *wrong.*

HASTY MORAL JUDGMENT

Psychologist Carl Rogers has observed that the single greatest barrier to meaningful communication between people is the tendency to respond with moral judgments. As we can see from the foregoing exchange between Yvonne and her instructor, hasty moral judgment also blocks objective analysis of a subject or concept.

Don't mistake my meaning here. I'm not for a moment suggesting that you should abandon your value system and regard all actions as equally defensible. Nor am I suggesting that considered moral judgments are to be avoided. After all, deep ethical convictions and principles are hallmarks of our very humanity. Achieving an objective attitude does not mean adopting a moral or ethical neutrality.

But the goals of analysis are understanding and insight. *Hasty* moral judgment blocks understanding and insight because it substitutes an emotional, judgmental label for calm analysis.

ANALYSIS

We left Yvonne venting her anger at the stupidity of the instructor, who had suggested that, if Yvonne could see advantages in being a social worker and yet not want to be one, she could safely consider reasons why a mother might decide to leave her family. But Yvonne only shook her head and cried, "Walking out on your husband and children is *wrong.*" This intriguing exchange continues:

INSTRUCTOR: Do you feel that being a social worker is wrong, too?

YVONNE: No, wrong for me, but not *wrong.* They're not the same thing at *all.*

INSTRUCTOR: Oh. And is being a runaway mother wrong for you?

YVONNE: Of course. But it's also *wrong* wrong.

INSTRUCTOR: *Wrong* wrong?

YVONNE (*with conviction*): *Wrong* wrong.

INSTRUCTOR: Do you mean *morally* wrong?

YVONNE: What else do you think I could have meant?

INSTRUCTOR: But being a social worker is not morally wrong?

YVONNE: No.

INSTRUCTOR: It's wrong for you. *Personally* wrong?

YVONNE: Yes.

INSTRUCTOR: So you are objecting to social work for *personal* reasons and to runaway mothers for *moral* reasons.

YVONNE (*happily*): Exactly! You're not as dense as I thought.

INSTRUCTOR: Thank you.

YVONNE: You're welcome.

INSTRUCTOR: May we return to the point?

YVONNE: Let's do.

INSTRUCTOR: You are objecting to runaway mothers on the grounds of *morality.* What do you mean by *moral* reasons?

YVONNE: Moral is moral. Right and wrong.

INSTRUCTOR: Are we going to start this again?

YVONNE: God, I hope not.

INSTRUCTOR: Exactly—God!

YVONNE: What?

INSTRUCTOR: When you refer to moral reasons, don't you actually have in mind *religious* sanctions against a wife forsaking her spouse and children?

YVONNE: Of course.

INSTRUCTOR: So you are objecting to runaway mothers on *religious* grounds.

YVONNE: Yes.

INSTRUCTOR: We could call this a *point of view.* You are citing an argument against such behavior from a *religious* point of view.

YVONNE: Yes.

INSTRUCTOR: Can you think of any other points of view from which objections can be found?

YVONNE (*brightly*): Sure!

INSTRUCTOR: For example?

YVONNE: The *social* point of view.

INSTRUCTOR: Yes?

YVONNE: Well, what do you think my parents and friends and neighbors at home would do if I ever walked out like that?

INSTRUCTOR: What?

YVONNE: They would die!

INSTRUCTOR: Really? How sad.

YVONNE: Not die. *Die!*

INSTRUCTOR: Die?

YVONNE: *Die!*

INSTRUCTOR: This again?

YVONNE: They would be shocked and talk about me.

INSTRUCTOR: Yes?

YVONNE: And it would get around.

INSTRUCTOR: Yes?

YVONNE: And the girls at church would whisper behind my back.

INSTRUCTOR: Yes?

YVONNE: And people would look at me like I was dirt.

INSTRUCTOR: Yes?

YVONNE (*bursting into tears*): Oh! I just couldn't stand it!

INSTRUCTOR (*handing Yvonne a Kleenex*): You're losing your detachment again.

YVONNE (*sniffling*): Sorry.

INSTRUCTOR: In other words, you could also argue against a mother's leaving from the point of view of the *social consequences* of such an action.

YVONNE: Oh boy!

INSTRUCTOR: You could show that, from a *social* point of view, she might suffer the consequences of gossip and condemnation, maybe even ostracism.

YVONNE: And that's not all. Think about the poor children.

INSTRUCTOR: What about them?

YVONNE: How would you have felt if *your* mother had run off when you were a child?

INSTRUCTOR: Umm . . .

YVONNE (*indignantly*): Terrible, that's how. Abandoned. You'd probably carry the emotional scars for the rest of your life.

INSTRUCTOR: From what perspective are you looking at the subject now?

YVONNE: Psychological effects on the children. If a woman brings a child into this world, she has a duty to care for it. When I think of a mother just taking off and leaving her little darling. . . . Oh, I can't stand it!

Once again, we must break into this emotion-charged scene with the cold voice of reason.

Yvonne, though far from objective, has been able to begin *analyzing* the topic. She is still against a mother's leaving her family, but she has progressed beyond hasty moral judgment, which blocked rational thought about the subject. She has come to realize that there are different *points of view* from which one can look at the matter.

POINTS OF VIEW

Imagine yourself trying to view a mansion surrounded by a high, dense hedge. The hedge has holes in it here and there, and you peer through one and then another and another. Each opening allows you to see only a small portion of the mansion. By the time you have looked through all the holes, or *points of view*, you will have an accurate conception of the nature and appearance of the mansion. But if you were asked to describe the mansion and looked through only one or two holes, you would probably be able to give only a very incomplete, or even inaccurate, description. For example, what if the hole you looked through allowed you to see only the servants' quarters? In that case, you might even deny that there was a mansion at all.

The first step Yvonne took was to realize that, in using the word "wrong," she was referring to the viewpoint labeled "religion"—she found that she could argue against a mother's leaving her family from the *religious* point of view.

After that, she moved on to another vantage point, the *social* point of view, and realized that her community's reaction to such behavior would be extremely negative.

Finally, she found a third perspective, that of *psychological effects* on the children.

So far, then, the points of view from which Yvonne has looked at the subject have allowed her to see only its *unfavorable* aspects (like the ugly parts of the mansion). But if she continues to move along the hedge searching for additional openings, she may find one or two points of view that give a different perspective on the subject. Let us return.

INSTRUCTOR: Earlier, you mentioned that social work wasn't for you, not because it was wrong, but just because you didn't find it appealing.

YVONNE: Yes.

INSTRUCTOR: It was not for you, *personally.*

YVONNE: Yes.

INSTRUCTOR: You were rejecting it from a *personal* point of view.

YVONNE (*impatiently*): Yes.

INSTRUCTOR: You are also criticizing runaway mothers from a *personal* point of view, and this view is largely determined by *religious sanctions* and *social consequences.*

YVONNE (*with a despairing sigh*): Yes.

INSTRUCTOR: But some people do not accept these religious sanctions and are willing to accept the social consequences you mention.

YVONNE: Oh! I hate people like that!

INSTRUCTOR: Really?

YVONNE: Really. Selfish, cold, heartless mothers. They don't care about anybody but themselves. The rest of the world can go hang, for all it matters to them.

INSTRUCTOR: You think all runaway mothers are like that?

YVONNE: Of course. No kind or loving woman would walk out on her family. No way.

STEREOTYPING

Yvonne is here manifesting an especially invidious block to logical thinking—stereotyping. To her way of thinking, *all* runaway mothers have the same characteristics. This is the first crucial and destructive aspect of stereotyping—a large number of unique persons who have only one thing in common are lumped together in a way that denies their individuality. Second, as Yvonne does, the stereotyper attributes to all members of the designated group certain traits in common, to the exclusion of all others (here these traits are selfishness, coldness, heartlessness, and uncaringness).

The net result of the stereotyping process is *dehumanization.* Instead of being recognized as a complex and unique individual, the stereotyped person is regarded as the sum of the few traits that comprise the stereotype.

INSTRUCTOR: Often, when you are trying to analyze a subject, it helps to *empathize* with the person who holds an opinion opposite to your own.

That is, put yourself in the place of a runaway mother and try to understand her situation and emotions and motives.

YVONNE: This country is going to the dogs.

INSTRUCTOR: Is that relevant?

YVONNE: No.

INSTRUCTOR: Try.

YVONNE: Well . . .

INSTRUCTOR: Yes?

YVONNE (*repressing a shudder*): Well . . . I suppose in some cases the woman might be scared.

INSTRUCTOR: Could you elaborate on that?

YVONNE (*growing more impassioned as she speaks*): Well, imagine what it would be like if she was married to a real ogre, maybe even a wife-beater, and she felt she just had to get away from him, but she knew that if she took the children he'd come after her and do terrible things to her and then take back the kids anyway. In a case like that, I don't see what other choice a woman would have, at least until she could get some legal protection, except to just run away.

INSTRUCTOR: Is there any other marriage situation that might justify a woman's leaving her family?

YVONNE: Well, I suppose in some cases, after years of marriage and waiting on others and always putting the needs of her husband and children first, a woman might come to feel that she was just disappearing as a person. She might feel she just had to break out and be herself. Let her husband and kids take care of themselves for a while. Let them do their own damned laundry, cook their own stupid meals, wash their own cruddy dishes. I mean, a person can take only so much slave work. Enough is enough. Let freedom ring. Down with male chauvinist exploiters. Sisterhood forever!

EMPATHY

Even though Yvonne is getting emotional again, she has taken a valuable step. She has looked at the subject from a *different point of view*. She has put herself in the place of someone who holds a point of view opposite her own and has tried to understand *that person's* situation and view of the subject. This has allowed her to achieve a *broader perspective*, a more nearly complete view of the subject. This has also enabled her to realize the *complexity* of the subject. She now sees that a simple right or wrong response is inadequate.

INSTRUCTOR (*mildly*): I would feel more comfortable if you would quit waving your fist in my face.

YVONNE (*blushing self-consciously and lowering her arm*): Oh, sorry about that. I got a bit carried away.

INSTRUCTOR (*glancing at her watch*): It's a quarter past the hour. Don't you think it might be a good idea to start working on your essay?

YVONNE (*starting for her seat*): I'll never be able to do it justice in just forty-five minutes.

SUMMARY

Thinking back over this scene, we can perceive the steps Yvonne took:

1. Confronted with the subject, she first had to set aside her emotional, subjective reactions in order to achieve *objectivity*.
2. Then she was able to begin *analysis* of the subject in order to gain *insight*.
3. This analysis involved:
   a. looking at the subject from various *points of view*
   b. *classifying* these points of view
   c. recognizing the *complexity* of the subject.

Throughout her analysis, she had to fight against the intrusion of such blocks to logical thinking as loss of objectivity, hasty moral judgment, and stereotyping. All of these blocks interfere with insight, which is the goal of analysis.

To understand points of view that differed from her own, Yvonne found it helpful to *empathize* with those people who held different attitudes in order to *broaden her perspective* on the subject and to *recognize its complexity*.

It is only at this point, *after* thoroughly analyzing the subject, that Yvonne was in a position to state a meaningful opinion on the subject.

A prejudice is any *irrationally held belief*, whether accurate or inaccurate. A prejudice differs from a meaningful opinion in this element of irrationality. The way a prejudiced person thinks might be summed up by this statement: "My mind's made up; don't confuse me with the facts."

Yvonne's feeling at the beginning of the scene that runaway mothers are "terrible" was a prejudice. By the end of the scene, Yvonne has developed a rationally held *opinion* concerning the subject. She still feels that for a mother to leave her family is a serious step to take, but now she has a broader and deeper understanding of the fundamental issues involved.

Represented in outline form, Yvonne's analysis looks like this:

I. Arguments against
   A. Religious sanctions
   B. Social consequences
   C. Psychological harm to children
II. Possible justifications
   A. Fear of an abusive husband
   B. Need for autonomy

Now Yvonne is in a position to formulate her thesis statement. She might write:

Thesis Statement A—A runaway mother violates the religious sanctity of marriage, faces almost certain social condemnation, and risks inflicting grave psychological trauma on her children. Some women, however, may have such fear of their husbands' retribution or such an overwhelming need for autonomy that "running away" is their only means of escape from an intolerable situation.

Thesis Statement A gives approximately the same weight to both major perspectives: arguments against and justifications. In this statement, Yvonne is being neutral.

She might, however, wish to indicate her own personal conviction, which is unsympathetic toward runaway mothers. She can do this, *while at the same time recognizing a point of view different from her own* (which she must do if she is to give a full and balanced picture of the subject), by conceding the possible justifications first and then stressing the overwhelming "negatives." In this case, her thesis statement might read as follows:

Thesis Statement B—It may be that some women feel they can escape an assaultive husband or assert their autonomy only by running away from their spouse and their children. But the costs of such a drastic action are tremendous. The runaway mother violates the sacred vows of marriage and exposes herself to social condemnation. Most grave of all, however, she runs the risk of inflicting serious and lasting psychological scars on her children.

ACKNOWLEDGE THE OPPOSITION

Do you see what's going on in the first part of Thesis Statement B? Yvonne is *conceding* the existence of a certain viewpoint that goes counter to her main argument. When you take a pro or con position on a controversial subject, this concession is called "acknowledging the opposition"—and it's crucial.

Say you're writing an essay that argues for or against legalized abortion, euthanasia, methadone maintenance programs, drafting women, or raising the sales tax. All of these are clearly two-sided issues. In other words, informed people have advanced reasonable, intelligent arguments favoring these practices and proposals, and informed people have advanced reasonable, intelligent arguments against these practices and proposals.

When you write a persuasive essay on such controversial issues as these, *be fair.*

Of course, your goal is to bring readers around to your view. But you will be much more likely to achieve this goal if readers who are initially uncommitted or opposed to your position feel that "the other side" has received a fair shake. If you ignore major arguments typically advanced by the opposition, readers are likely to respond by ignoring your arguments.

YVONNE AND ROCK NORMAL
A TALE OF OLD ROLES REVERSED

Rock Normal is a classmate of Yvonne's in English composition. Clean-cut, blonde-haired, broad-shouldered, and standing 6'3" in his socks, Rock, an ex-high school football player, cuts a handsome if not particularly high-brow figure. His protective instincts were aroused at the sight of Yvonne's distress on the first day of class, when the instructor assigned that "immoral" theme. A few class meetings later, when he noticed Yvonne had received an *A* (compared to his *D +*), other instincts were aroused as well. Now, in the third week of the term, with an essay due tomorrow, Rock has asked Yvonne over to his apartment. Still indignant about the first theme assignment, Rock has decided to write an essay showing the sanctity of marriage. But somehow he doesn't seem to be making much progress.

When we join them, Rock is standing before the couch in the living room of his apartment, reading the opening paragraph of his essay to Yvonne.

ROCK (*with expressive gestures as he reads*): Marriage is a noble union made in heaven, blessed by God, and hallowed by man. It takes two lonely, separate persons and makes them one and indivisible, for better or for worse, in sickness and in health, forever. It provides a warm, peaceful, happy, loving nest in which to raise the young that are its natural offspring. Yes, marriage leads to the joys of family life. It provides a happy home in which can be heard the joyful lilt of children's voices, the light patter of little feet, the excited laughter of little angels at play. Marriage is a wonderful thing.

ROCK (*with a smug smile*): What do you think?

YVONNE: I think you want to get married.

ROCK (*gruffly*): I mean about the paragraph?

YVONNE: I think it's lousy.

ROCK (*indignantly*): "Lousy"? It's beautiful!

YVONNE (*mildly*): Lousy.

ROCK (*recalling it was Yvonne who got the A*): How come?

YVONNE: I'll show you. (*She picks up his paper and pretends to read.*) Marriage is a clever snare conceived in hell, hexed by the devil, and perpetrated on unsuspecting women by conniving men. It takes two separate, happy persons and chains them together, one and indivisible— until they get divorced—in a misery of boredom. It provides a steaming, tension-ridden, hate-filled cauldron in which to boil the unfortunate children who are its accidental by-product. It provides a one-bedroom furnished cage in which to be tormented by the howls of colicky infants, the stench of wet diapers, and the screaming, tearful quarrels of selfish offspring. Yes, marriage is a wonderful thing.

ROCK (*collapsing dumbfounded onto the sofa*): How could such horrible thoughts ever get into such a pretty head?

YVONNE (*putting her hand on Rock's shoulder and looking at the dandruff in the part of his hair*): I don't know, they just did.

ROCK: Mother would just die.

YVONNE (*relenting*): If it's any help, my paragraph is just as lousy as yours.

ROCK (*beginning to brighten*): Really?

YVONNE: Yes, neither one actually says a thing.

ROCK: How come?

YVONNE: Both are simply *reactions* to the subject. Both are *subjective* responses, both are full of *hasty moral judgment* and *either–or thinking,* both contain *implied assertions.* Neither one is a meaningful *analysis* of the subject.

ROCK (*gazing admiringly into Yvonne's eyes*): You analyze it for me; I'll listen.

YVONNE: Whose theme is this, anyway?

ROCK: But you're so smart. Please?

YVONNE (*secretly flattered, but with pretended reluctance*): Well, okay. (*Rock happily sprawls out on the couch.*) Now, the subject you are writing on is "Marriage." So, you must first of all:

1. Avoid getting *personally involved.* You must be *objective.*
2. Avoid *either–or thinking.*
3. Avoid *hasty moral judgment.*

ROCK (*digging in his ear*): Right.

YVONNE: Then you can begin to *analyze* the subject. The purpose of analysis is understanding. To understand, you have to *recognize the complexity* of the subject. To recognize the complexity of the subject, you must look at it from various *points of view.*

ROCK (*sleepily*): Sure thing.

YVONNE: All right, then. What's one point of view from which we can look at marriage?

ROCK (*dreamily*): Love! Love and marriage go together like a horse and carriage.

YVONNE: False analogy.

ROCK: What?

YVONNE: A false analogy is a comparison between two unlike subjects that ignores basic differences between them. Love is not the same as a horse, and marriages and carriages aren't much alike either.

ROCK: Oh.

YVONNE: The analogy also involves an implied assertion.

ROCK: Huh?

YVONNE: Through your comparison of love and marriage to a horse and carriage, you are really asserting that there is a necessary connection between loving and getting married.

ROCK (*indignantly*): But, there is. Ask any man. If he loves a woman, he wants to marry her.

YVONNE (*with conviction*): Cultural conditioning plus chauvinistic chattel mentality.

ROCK (*hopelessly*): I'm lost.

YVONNE (*patiently*): When you say "love," you are describing a *reason* why people get married, right?

ROCK: Of course.

YVONNE: So, you are looking at marriage from the point of view of why people get married, from the point of view of *motives* for marriage.

ROCK: Yes.

YVONNE: But, from this point of view, are there any other common or possible motives besides love?

ROCK (*turning to Yvonne, who is sitting beside him on the couch, and tickling her under her chin*): Coochy, coochy, coo!

YVONNE (*turning her head away*): Right. A couple could marry in order to raise children.

ROCK (*with visions of Yvonne as a registered nurse*): Or to get economic security.

YVONNE: Or emotional security.

ROCK: Or because it was expected.

YVONNE: Or because they wanted to live together and didn't dare without being married.

ROCK (*pleased with himself*): I get the idea!

YVONNE: Bravo! So, from this point of view of *motivation,* we have six reasons why people may marry: because they love each other, because they want children, because they want economic security, because they want emotional security, because it is expected, because they want to live together.

ROCK (*losing interest*): Yes.

YVONNE: Is there any other point of view from which marriage can be considered?

ROCK: I don't know.

YVONNE: Well, think.

ROCK (*starting to get up*): Let's go to a movie. There's a double feature at the Center—*King Kong* and *King Kong Meets Godzilla.*

YVONNE: Sit down!

ROCK (*subsiding*): All right already.

YVONNE: We call marriage an "institution," don't we?

ROCK (*subdued*): Yes.

YVONNE: Is the Democratic party an institution?

ROCK: Yes.

YVONNE: Classify it.

ROCK (*blinking his eyes*): What?

YVONNE: Put it into the class or group of institutions to which it belongs. What *type* of institution is it?

ROCK: A *political* institution.

YVONNE: And the Catholic Church?

ROCK: A *religious* institution.

YVONNE: And the World Bank?

ROCK: An *economic* institution.

YVONNE: And marriage?

ROCK: A *social* institution.

YVONNE: Good boy. So, we can look at marriage from the point of view of a social institution. The Democratic party, the Catholic Church, and the World Bank have certain *functions* as institutions. Marriage, too, has certain functions as a *social* institution.

ROCK: Name one.

YVONNE: You name one.

ROCK: I can't.

YVONNE: Think.

ROCK (*after a moment, tentatively*): Well, just imagine what might happen without the institution of marriage.

YVONNE: What?

ROCK (*getting more and more worked up as he talks*): It's terrible. The world would be full of unwed mothers carrying their poor babies from door to door, looking for a home. A woman might give a man the best years of her life, and then the jerk could just kick her out into a dark, cold winter night and slam the door. And she couldn't do a thing. She might starve or have to go to work as a washerwoman to feed her children. A man could will all his money to any young hussy he wanted to and leave his children to suffer. And no one would be responsible for raising the children and clothing them and feeding them. Oh, it's terrible!

YVONNE (*putting her arms around Rock to comfort him*): Get hold of yourself.

ROCK (*sniffling*): Sorry.

YVONNE: So, we can look at marriage from the point of view of its social functions.

ROCK (*drying his eyes*): Yes.

YVONNE: One of the social functions of the institution of marriage, then, is to provide for children. The institution of marriage ensures that someone will be responsible for the feeding, clothing, and rearing of the young.

ROCK: Yes.

YVONNE: Marriage as a social institution may also, as you suggest, help provide the marriage partners with the emotional security they may need to best perform their role as parents.

ROCK: Yes.

YVONNE: Okay. Is there still another point of view from which you can look at marriage?

ROCK (*sitting up and laughing*): Well, when you sign the marriage license and say "I do," you're hooked!

YVONNE (*trying to keep from shuddering*): I can feel the barb in my guts, like a fish. But what exactly do you mean, "hooked"?

ROCK (*laughing*): You can't get away, sister!

YVONNE: Why not?

ROCK (*smugly*): You can't break the contract.

YVONNE: Exactly. A contract. From what point of view are you looking at marriage now?

ROCK: From the *legal* point of view. If you try anything, I'll call my father's lawyer.

YVONNE: You're right. From a legal point of view, marriage is a contract between two people in which both assume certain obligations to each other and to the offspring of the marriage. Thus, a man or woman may be lawfully penalized for failure to meet the obligations of the contract.

ROCK (*gleefully rubbing his hands*): And don't forget that the woman has to take the kids and go on welfare if she ever tries to weasel out of the deal!

YVONNE: What a lovely thought.

ROCK: But true! But true!

YVONNE: I think I'd like to get back to your essay.

ROCK (*smugly*): I want to look at the legal point of view some more!

YVONNE (*ignoring him*): We have now looked at marriage from a personal, a social, and a legal point of view. Or, to put it another way, from the point of view of:

1. The *motives* of the couple who marry.
2. The *social functions* of the institution of marriage.
3. The *legal* aspects of marriage.

ROCK (*inching closer*): Umm.

YVONNE: To sum up, then, we have found that there are at least six motives for marriage: love, a desire for children, a desire for economic security, a desire for emotional security, a desire to conform, and a desire to live together. Marriage as a social institution has at least two functions: to provide for the rearing and socialization of children and to provide the marriage partners with emotional security they need to best perform their role as parents. Finally, marriage is a legal contract between the marriage partners in which both undertake certain responsibilities and that provides for penalties if these responsibilities are not met.

ROCK (*getting passionate*): You're great!

YVONNE (*moving his hands away*): It's so nice to feel appreciated.

SUMMARY

Although Rock seems to have a long way to go, Yvonne has clearly benefited from the illuminating exchange with her instructor in the earlier dialogue. In outline form, Yvonne's analysis of "marriage" looks like this:

I. Motives for Marriage
   A. Love
   B. Desire for children
   C. Desire for economic security
   D. Desire for emotional security
   E. Desire to conform
   F. Desire to live together

II. Social Functions of the Institution of Marriage
   A. To provide for the rearing and socialization of children
   B. To provide the emotional security the partners may need to best perform their role as parents

III. Legal Aspects of Marriage
   A. Contract in which both parties agree to fulfill certain obligations
   B. Contract providing for penalties if obligations are not fulfilled

Full development of all these aspects of marriage would probably be impossible in a short essay. Rock might choose to restrict his discussion to any one of the three major points of view. However, if he did decide to write on the subject as analyzed, without limiting it, his thesis should reflect all three major points of view from which the subject was examined. And his thesis should be carefully formulated to indicate the order and emphasis of the whole essay:

Thesis Statement A—Although marriage is both a legally binding contract and an institution with significant social functions, it is most often entered into because of the personal needs of the two people involved. (This thesis statement puts the emphasis of the essay on the personal motives that cause people to marry.)

Thesis Statement B—Marriage is a legally binding contract that is often entered into because of the personal needs of the marriage partners. However, it is as a social institution that it is most significant. (This thesis statement obviously puts the emphasis on marriage as a social institution.)

Thesis Statement C—People tend to regard marriage as a means of satisfy-ing personal needs or as a socially important institution. However, marriage is also a legal contract between two parties involving mutual obligations and responsibilities. (This thesis statement emphasizes marriage as a legally binding contract.)

NOTE: Analysis is a formal technique for exploring a subject and organiz-ing your findings. But the results of analysis may be expressed in as informal and lively a fashion as you desire or deem appropriate to your subject and audience. Thus, in a more informal essay, Thesis Statement C might read:

Some see marriage as a quick fix for all their personal needs. Others seem to regard it as the last bastion between order and social chaos. But I see it as just one more business deal.

No? How about this?

When it comes to marriage, you can be romantic, conservative, or realistic. The romantic says "I do" and sees bliss; the conservative says "I do" and sees social stability; the realist says "I do" and wishes they gave out a warranty with the rice.

Oh well . . . at least you get the idea. After all, what's Paul Simon's song "Fifty Ways to Leave Your Lover" except extended analysis? Analysis is an investigative tool. How you pound the nail is up to you.

ANALYSIS AS DISCOVERY

It can be argued that analysis and classification are *the basic* reasoning processes—imposing order on chaos, revealing patterns where none were perceived before, making experience manageable. Thus, analysis can serve not only to guide your investigation into a subject you are already knowledgeable about but can also help you *discover* new pat-terns, relationships, and perspectives.

In his well-known book *I'm OK—You're OK*, psychologist Thomas A. Harris describes how he came to realize that the human psyche could be analyzed from three perspectives, which he classified as *parent, child,* and *adult.* Both Harris's book and a widely employed method of therapy —transactional analysis—resulted from this analytical discovery.

In her seminal study, *On Death and Dying,* physician Elisabeth

Kübler-Ross identifies five stages in the response of terminally ill people to their own impending death: (1) denial and isolation, (2) anger, (3) bargaining, (4) depression, and finally (5) acceptance. This analytic insight has had profound therapeutic value, helping the dying and those close to them come to terms with the traumas of terminal illness. And, of course, it's difficult to imagine how we could comprehend the human psyche without Freud's analytical divisions: *id, ego,* and *superego.*

Most of the time, naturally, our analytical insights will not have such dramatic consequences as those just described, but they can be fresh and useful nonetheless.

HIGHLIGHTS

- *Hasty* moral judgment blocks understanding and insight because it substitutes an emotional, judgmental label for calm analysis.
- The net result of stereotyping is *dehumanization.*
- A prejudice is any *irrationally held belief,* whether accurate or inaccurate.
- If you ignore major arguments typically advanced by the opposition, readers are likely to respond by ignoring your arguments.
- Analysis can serve not only to guide your investigation of a subject you are already knowledgeable about but also to help you *discover* new patterns, relationships, and perspectives.

APPLICATIONS: ANALYSIS IN ACTION

Choose one or more of the following subjects. Then:

1. Analyze the subject.
2. Construct a topic outline of your analysis.
3. Write out at least two thesis statements for each subject you analyzed. Each thesis on a given subject should emphasize a different point of view, as illustrated on pages 22–23.

COLLEGE LIFE	GENERAL
College	Advertising
Dormitories	Travel
Study habits	Health

Roommates
Required courses
Liberal education
Specialization
Grades
Examinations
Instructors

SOCIAL LIFE
Drinking
Friends
Fads
Parties
Co-workers

Automobiles
Divorce
Hit tunes
Crash diets
Hobbies
Pets
Highway safety
Police
Parents
Factory work
In-laws
Movies
TV
Videos
Graffiti
Drugs

APPLICATIONS: ANALYSIS AS DISCOVERY

Select a common situation, location, or activity familiar to most people, and observe it with fresh eyes, *analytically.* See whether you can *discover* and *classify* distinct patterns of behavior, or character types, or whatever. Then explain your new perception in an analytical essay.

Some possibilities:

People in elevators
People riding escalators
Schoolchildren on a playground
People in a bar
Workers in a factory or office
Students in a cafeteria

People in a doctor's waiting room
Smokers
Men in a barber shop
Women in a beauty parlor
Students in a lecture hall
People in a subway car

SECTION TWO

BLOCKS TO LOGICAL THINKING

In order to reason clearly and dispassionately, we must struggle against truly elemental forces: the powerful conditioning of our culture; the sometimes deeply buried needs and fears of our psyche; the pervasive influence of the very language with which we conceptualize and articulate our thoughts.

Each of these three forces—cultural, psychological, and linguistic—affects how we think and how we reason in subtle and complex ways. They are the well-spring from which illogic ultimately flows.

In the chapters that follow, we explore the nature of these elemental forces and discuss ways to overcome their often pernicious influence.

1

Cultural Conditioning

> The trouble ain't that people are ignorant;
> it's that they "know" so much that ain't so.
>
> JOSH BILLINGS

Many people regard the following statements as sound, "logical" arguments:

Drinking in college dormitories should not be permitted because intoxicated students would disturb others.

Government spending must be cut so we can achieve a balanced budget.

Parents should think twice before getting a divorce because of the dire effects on the children.

Children should be encouraged to say their prayers because saying prayers will strengthen their religious faith.

Capitalism is desirable because it encourages free enterprise.

Apparently each of these statements contains two assertions, which we can call *conclusion* and *reason*, respectively. For example:

Conclusion: Capitalism is *desirable.*
Reason: Capitalism *encourages free enterprise.*
Conclusion: Children *should be encouraged to say their prayers.*
Reason: Saying prayers *will strengthen their religious faith.*

So, if you are writing a paragraph and one of these statements is your topic sentence, your job would appear to be to show how and why capitalism encourages free enterprise or how and why saying prayers strengthens religious faith. And if you do show how and why your *reason* is true, the *conclusion* would seem to follow. But the *conclusion does not follow.*

IMPLIED ASSERTION

The conclusion does not follow because each of these statements contains not two but *three* assertions. This third assertion we shall call an *implied assertion* because it is *implied* by the other two. The point to remember about this implied assertion is that it is *hidden*. It is not spelled out like the other two. Nevertheless, it is still there.

For example, take the statement "Capitalism is desirable because it encourages free enterprise." The conclusion "Capitalism is desirable" does not follow from the assertion that "Capitalism encourages free enterprise" (reason) unless it is *also* true that "Free enterprise is desirable" (implied assertion).

"But," you may say, *"everybody* knows that free enterprise is desirable."

No.

Communists obviously don't believe that free enterprise is desirable. Socialists such as those in England who have supported nationalization of key industries obviously don't believe that free enterprise is desirable. Americans who set up communes and Utopian communities in which everybody shared equally didn't believe that free enterprise was desirable.

Furthermore, the term "free enterprise" is an empty abstraction (see Chapter Three) that may have different meanings to different people. A thief who picks your pocket is exercising free enterprise. So is the man who poisons his wife to collect the insurance. So is the doctor who refuses to treat a dying person until assured of payment. Is such free enterprise desirable?

Once you have written out the *implied assertion,* you can *concretize* it to test its accuracy. But the danger is that you may never even realize that a given statement or argument contains a hidden assertion. The reason you may completely overlook the existence of an implied assertion can be traced to *cultural conditioning.*

CULTURALLY CONDITIONED ASSUMPTIONS

We are, to a large degree, creatures of our particular age. We grow up in a certain "climate of opinion." And this climate of opinion determines the form of many of our *attitudes* and *values.* These attitudes and values tend to change rather slowly. There is a tendency for them to lag behind changes in social structure, economic realities, scientific discoveries, and so forth. Thus, many people have values and attitudes that don't reflect the reality of the world they live in. The result is an inability to think rationally and objectively about many subjects.

Let's look at some examples:

Individuality—Most people in America "believe in" individuality. In other words, it is a value toward which they have a favorable attitude. Yet these same people may be quite critical of those who assert their individuality in socially disapproved ways. They may criticize the dropout who found school irrelevant. They may regard as perverted or degenerate people who assert their individual preference for homosexuality or bisexuality. They may condemn people who are aggressive in pursuit of their ambitions.

The American Dream—Many people in America today believe that, if you work hard and save your money, you can become wealthy. They believe that it is possible, through hard work and education, for an average citizen to advance "from rags to riches." Of course, once upon a time we had a wide-open, laissez-faire economic system, taxes were low, population was light, and the resources of the country were largely undeveloped. A belief in the American dream made some sense then, though not much.

But today, American society has changed. It is highly structured; the population is relatively dense; taxes are high; opportunities to "make a killing" are few; upward mobility is limited. Today the American dream, the belief that hard work and integrity will always lead to wealth and power, is questionable indeed, yet it is still widely believed in.

War—Americans, prior to the second half of the twentieth century (and with the possible exception of their own Revolutionary War), had experienced only one kind of war—war in which armies faced armies along a "front." When the armies of one nation were no longer capable of resisting the advance of the armies of another nation, they were "defeated"—they surrendered and peace followed. Until the latter part of the Vietnam War, there was no widespread recognition of the essential difference between a conventional "front" war and modern guerrilla warfare. Americans learned the falsity of this culturally conditioned assumption at immense cost.

Progress—Many Americans (and many citizens of other nations, too) are still firmly committed to the idea of "progress" as measured by an increasing gross national product, a higher standard of living, a growing population, and so forth. The concept of a "zero-growth economy" is abhorrent to many, if not most, Americans. Yet ecologically minded scientists have demonstrated that continued exponential growth in population and resource consumption is dangerous and destructive and could lead to worldwide economic collapse. Nevertheless, the "growth is good" mentality continues to predominate.

The point of citing these examples of culturally conditioned values and attitudes is simply this:

Because we live in a particular country, in a particular part of the world, in a particular age; because we were raised in a particular class and educated in a particular educational system, *we possess a large collection of attitudes and values whose accuracy, truth, or merit we have probably never questioned.*

These attitudes and values can be called *assumptions* because we *assume* them to be accurate. We don't question them; we probably don't even see them as open to question.

One of the things education is all about is learning to question our assumptions. But we obviously can't question them until we train ourselves to recognize them.

When you realize that you are making an assumption, write it out in the form of an assertion. Then test the accuracy of the assertion by *concretizing* it. Many culturally conditioned assumptions, like those discussed on pages 31–32, involve empty abstractions. In other words, they tend to be vague and general. Thus it is especially important to bring them down to concrete instances. To illustrate:

Conclusion and Reason: Drinking should not be allowed in college dormitories because intoxicated students would disturb others.

Assumption (stated as assertion): If people drink, they will become intoxicated and rowdy.

Concretization: Do I become intoxicated every time I drink? Do all the people I know who are allowed to drink become intoxicated every time they drink? Does permission to drink in dorms mean permission to become drunk and disorderly?

When you state and concretize your various assumptions in this way, you will undoubtedly retain some as accurate, reject some as inaccurate, and modify others to conform more closely to reality. In examining your assumptions, you will be converting them into rationally held opinions. Instead of your mind being a passive, uncritical receptacle for every half-baked notion floating around in the general culture, it will become an active, questioning intelligence.

The unexamined life is not worth living, Socrates observed. It is equally true that the unquestioned assumption is not worth having. The "obstinate obstetrician" whom Yvonne encounters in the following dialogue is one of the unenlightened.

Yvonne and the Obstinate Obstetrician

Only in soap operas and *Clear Thinking for Composition* do events march forward with such breathtaking speed. Since the last episode, Yvonne has married a fellow named C. S. Rott, which stands for *C*ollege *S*tudent who has *R*ead *T*his *T*ext.

Yvonne is now three months pregnant, and she and C. S. have decided that they want to use the Lamaze method of natural childbirth. Yvonne is about to communicate this decision to her obstetrician.

YVONNE: Doctor, C. S. and I have decided that we want to have a natural childbirth, and I want C. S. to be with me during delivery.

OBSTETRICIAN (*incredulously*): What?

YVONNE: C. S. and I have decided that we want . . .

OBSTETRICIAN: I heard what you said. You're repeating yourself. Just like a woman.

YVONNE (*indignantly*): That's a sexist stereotype.

OBSTETRICIAN (*emphatically*): I meant, "What nonsense."

YVONNE: So it's okay with you?

OBSTETRICIAN: No.

YVONNE (*ignoring him*): And I don't want you to administer any anesthetics. It's been shown that receiving anesthetics during childbirth can reduce the child's oxygen supply and possibly cause mental retardation.

OBSTETRICIAN: You'll scream.

YVONNE (*firmly*): I doubt it. I'm going to take lessons and do breathing exercises. And C. S. will be there to coach me. Besides, the most uncomfortable part is during labor, not delivery. Since most women with normal pregnancies are not anesthetized during labor, why should they be anesthetized during delivery?

OBSTETRICIAN: You've been reading too many books.

YVONNE (*reasonably*): Don't you think a woman should know what to expect and how to cope with it?

OBSTETRICIAN (*in a fatherly tone*): That's what I'm here for, honey. You just leave it all to me.

YVONNE: But it's *my* baby and *my* childbirth, not yours. I want to be conscious and aware. And C. S. wants to share this experience with me.

OBSTETRICIAN: You don't know what you're talking about. Think of all the blood and other stuff. Some husbands have been so turned off that they have lost all sexual interest in their wives. You don't want that to happen, now, do you?

YVONNE (*decisively*): C. S. and I have discussed this. We believe that birth is beautiful, not ugly. And we want to share it, together.

OBSTETRICIAN: Your husband may faint. I've got enough to do without having a hysterical husband on my hands.

YVONNE (*proudly*): C. S. won't faint or get hysterical. He's a very rational person. And another thing, I don't want to be shaved or to have an enema. Shaving the pubic hair can actually increase a woman's chance of infection because of razor nicks, and enemas have no proven value whatsoever.

OBSTETRICIAN: Young lady, which of us is the doctor here?

YVONNE: You are.

OBSTETRICIAN: And which of us has delivered hundreds of babies?

YVONNE: You have.

OBSTETRICIAN: And which of us spent four years in medical school?

YVONNE: You did.

OBSTETRICIAN: And which of us knows how hospitals operate?

YVONNE: You do.

OBSTETRICIAN (*smugly*): Okay. So which of us knows what's best for you?

YVONNE (*with conviction*): I do. It's my baby and my childbirth, and I have the right to have a say in it.

OBSTETRICIAN (*with finality*): Impossible. You'll do it my way or not at all.

YVONNE: No. I'll do it the best way.

OBSTETRICIAN: Then you'll have to do it without me.

YVONNE: Fine! You're just a culturally conditioned, expediency-oriented old fogy!

We can scarcely blame Yvonne for lapsing into name calling, for the obstetrician refuses to question, or even regard as open to question, the "knock-her-out-and-drag-it-out" approach to childbirth that he learned in medical school. Implicit in his comments are such culturally conditioned assumptions as these:

Delivery of a child is solely the doctor's business and should be conducted in that fashion most convenient to the doctor.

Without anesthetics a woman in labor will inevitably lose control.

Husbands don't belong in the delivery room.

Established hospital routine is right and must be followed.

As you can see from this list, a culturally conditioned assumption is not just any sort of assertion—it's a *blanket generalization.* So when we speak of an "implied assertion," we're talking about a *hidden generalization*. And that generalization must be true without exception if the conclusion supported by it is to follow.

Before we leave the subject of cultural conditioning, we should take a brief look at three related matters that also block logical thinking: *hasty moral judgment, compartmentalization,* and *either–or thinking.*

HASTY MORAL JUDGMENT

The tendency to make a *hasty moral judgment* about a subject is probably *the* most ingrained block to logical thinking and *the* greatest barrier to meaningful communication and understanding. A hasty, emotion-laden moral judgment bears the same relation to a reasoned value judgment that a prejudice bears to an informed opinion. Both prejudices and hasty moral judgments are essentially nonrational; both are signs of self-righteousness and intolerance; both substitute preconception for perception; and both conflict with the primary goals of logical thinking, which are insight and understanding.

We have a strong tendency in our society to label actions and ideas according to whether they lie in the Devil's camp or in God's. Perhaps this tendency can be traced to our Puritan heritage—who knows? What is important is to resist it. We should fight this tendency to make hasty moral judgments because the tendency blocks logical thinking. Analysis attempts to understand what something *is,* and hasty moral judgment prevents such understanding.

Although Yvonne's doctor was unable to question his culturally conditioned attitudes toward childbirth, at least he didn't condemn Yvonne with self-righteous moral judgments. Think for a moment of what would happen to medicine (and to your willingness to see a doctor) if doctors responded to their patients with *hasty moral judgment* rather than attempting to *understand.*

The Moralistic Medics

SCENE: *Clinic in a middle-sized town. Various rooms accommodate specialists in different fields.—*JOHN ACNE, *a young man of nineteen whose face is covered with zits, is entering the dermatologist's office.*

JOHN ACNE (*hesitantly*): Uh . . . Doctor . . .

DERMATOLOGIST (*interrupting him*): My God! Just look at you! What a mess! You look like a freak!

JOHN ACNE (*hiding his face behind his hands*): I'm sorry.

DERMATOLOGIST (*pulling his hands away*): Didn't I tell you to stop eating sweets? Didn't I?

JOHN ACNE (*in a weak voice*): Yes.

DERMATOLOGIST (*shaking his fist*): Well, why didn't you? What kind of slob are you anyway?

JOHN ACNE (*unconsciously scratching his face*): I tried . . .

DERMATOLOGIST: And just look at you, picking away. You make me sick!

We now move to another obstetrician's office.

MARY PREGNANT (*a young woman of seventeen in her fourth month of pregnancy. She wears no wedding ring.*): Hello, Doctor, I want to get a checkup to see how my baby's doing.

OBSTETRICIAN (*looking at the third finger of Mary's left hand*): Where's your wedding band?

MARY PREGNANT: I decided my boyfriend was immature, so I refused to marry him.

OBSTETRICIAN (*jumping up from behind his desk and glaring down at Mary*): What! Not married? Pregnant and not married?

MARY PREGNANT (*mildly*): Yes, Doctor.

OBSTETRICIAN (*ignoring her comment*): And you expect me to examine you? You expect me to dirty my hands by touching a fallen woman? (*He raises his arm and points dramatically.*) Away, wanton creature! Don't darken my door again!

Obviously, both of these physicians wreak havoc on their patients. Similarly, people who indulge in hasty moral judgment in their writing wreak havoc on the process of logical thinking and dispassionate analysis.

You should approach any subject in the same way that a competent physician approaches a patient. Indeed, a given subject of investigation is to your intelligence as a patient is to a doctor. The doctor's goal is to gain insight into, and to understand the nature of, the patient's physical state. Your goal is to gain insight into and to understand the various aspects of your subject. In both cases, hasty moral judgment makes achieving the goal of understanding and insight impossible.

Do not misconstrue these observations to mean you should not have strong ethical convictions about what is right and wrong, good and bad. But moral judgment should be deliberate rather than precipitous and should follow reflective analysis rather than precede it.

COMPARTMENTALIZATION

Compartmentalization allows us to *say* we believe one thing while *acting* as though we believe something else, without perceiving any contradiction. It allows us to make a general statement that is incompatible with a more specific statement, without perceiving any contradiction.

For example, a student wrote a theme on euthanasia in which he took the position that mercy killing should not be allowed because only God has the right to take a human life. A week or so later he wrote a theme on capital punishment in which he argued that the death penalty should be used to punish the perpetrators of a wide range of crimes. He saw no contradiction.

Another student wrote that welfare was a big rip-off of the working middle class by "lazy parasites" and that only the sick and disabled should receive assistance from federal programs. At the time she wrote this, she was herself collecting food stamps.

There are two principal ways to reduce compartmentalization:

1. Trace out the basic principle that is implied by a given belief that you hold.
2. Concretize your belief to determine whether there are exceptions to it on the level of specific instances.

Compartmentalization thrives on absolutes. When people maintain the truth of numerous absolutes, they *have* to compartmentalize to prevent reality—concrete instances, everyday experiences—from exposing the falseness of their beliefs. Such persons may tell a daughter, "Never marry a man who drinks," yet they admire and respect numerous people who drink. They may maintain that "A man who won't look you straight in the eye can't be trusted" and yet trust implicitly several men who have never looked them straight in the eye. They may maintain that "Motherhood is sacred" and yet give evidence in court to show why a certain mother is unfit to retain custody of her children.

Such people have safely insulated their culturally conditioned values and attitudes from the danger of being modified by reality. However, they scarcely strike us as persons to admire for their clarity of thought.

EITHER–OR THINKING

Either–or thinking is thinking that *ignores the complexity* of a subject. We are all familiar with the statement "The more I learn, the less I know." What this means, of course, is that the more we learn, the less sure we tend to become that we "know the truth" about various matters. Put more precisely, we come to realize that there is no "Truth," but rather many "truths" about most matters, depending on how we look at them.

There are many reasons for the prevalence of either–or thinking. One reason is the desire all persons have for certainty, and it is much easier to be certain about a matter if one ignores the complexities, the subtleties, the exceptions. A second reason is the tendency to apply the logic of mutual exclusiveness to abstractions as well as to objects. And a third reason, not to be underestimated, is the essentially antithetical nature of our language, which encourages us to think in terms of "opposites."

Because either–or thinking is such a major block to objective and sound reasoning, these three causes merit further examination.

1. *Intolerance of ambiguity*—Many people have a strong need for certainty. They need to feel that they "know the truth" about a subject or issue, and they want that "truth" to be clear-cut and unambiguous. Professor James G. Martin believes that the following set of statements effectively measures a person's relative tolerance or intolerance of ambiguity. If you wish to test yourself, circle the appropriate response to the left of each statement. (*SA*, strongly agree; *A*, agree; *U*, undecided; *D*, disagree; *SD*, strongly disagree.)

SA	A	U	D	SD	There are two kinds of people in the world: the weak and the strong.
SA	A	U	D	SD	A person is either 100 percent American or he isn't.
SA	A	U	D	SD	Either a person knows the answer to a question or he doesn't.
SA	A	U	D	SD	You can classify almost all people as either honest or crooked.

(SA) A U D SD First impressions are very important.

SA A (U) D SD It doesn't take very long to find out whether you
can trust a person.

SA A U D (SD) There is only one right way to do anything.

According to Professor Martin, a person who responds "agree" or "strongly agree" to most of these statements tends "to think and react in terms of dichotomized absolutes and rigidly exclusive categories."[1] In plain English, a person who agrees with the foregoing statements is probably prone to either–or thinking.

2. *The logic of mutual exclusiveness*—Common sense tells us that things are mutually exclusive: a bird is not a bee; a bee is not a blimp. In the everyday world of external, physical reality, it is true that two different objects cannot occupy the same space at the same time or be two different objects simultaneously. For example, if there is a solid block of wood 3 inches square sitting on your desk, there cannot be a block of plastic 3 inches square sitting in the same place at the same time; and if the block of wood is there, it cannot be simultaneously a block of plastic—they are *mutually exclusive.* But when this type of logic is applied to *concepts* such as democracy and justice; or to *states of mind* such as love and hate; or to human *institutions, issues,* and *behavior,* it is absolutely false.

Nevertheless, many people apply a false logic to their thoughts and emotions, a logic applicable only to external, physical objects. They believe that if they feel anger or hate toward someone, they cannot simultaneously love that person; that if men and women are to be held accountable for their actions, such actions cannot be simultaneously regarded as the outcome of social or environmental forces; that if welfare is abused by some recipients, it cannot be simultaneously unabused by most recipients.

This unwarranted extension of "common sense" logic inevitably leads to the oversimplification of complex issues and to either–or thinking. The answer to welfare fraud, such a person might argue, is *either* to weed out all the cheaters *or* to abolish the system. For people who reason in this way, no middle ground is acceptable.

3. *The antithetical nature of our language*—Our language provides us with a virtually inexhaustible supply of polar opposites: *conservative–liberal, happy–sad, intelligent–dumb, work–play, love–hate, good–bad,*

guilty–innocent, drunk–sober, hard–soft, true–false—the list could go on and on. The ready availability of these antonyms subtly affects the way we reason, encouraging us to think in terms of "either–or." Furthermore, as linguist Clyde Kluckhohn observed:

> Aristotelian logic teaches us that something [*either*] is *or* isn't. Such a statement is often false to reality, for *both–and* is more often true than *either–or.* . . . Actual experience does not present clear-cut entities like "good" and "bad," "mind" and "body"; the sharp split remains verbal.[2]

In short, the very structure of our language, a part of our cultural heritage, encourages us to think and reason in terms of oversimplified and reality-distorting opposites.

HIGHLIGHTS

- We possess a large number of (culturally conditioned) attitudes and values whose accuracy, truth, or merit we have probably never questioned.
- The tendency to make a *hasty moral judgment* about a subject is probably *the most* ingrained block to logical thinking and the greatest barrier to meaningful communication and understanding.
- Moral judgment should be deliberate rather than precipitous, and it should follow analysis rather than precede it.
- Compartmentalization allows us to *say* we believe one thing while acting as though we believe something else, without perceiving any contradiction. It allows us to make a general statement that is incompatible with a more specific statement, without perceiving any contradiction.
- "Aristotelian logic teaches us that something [*either*] is *or* isn't. Such a statement is often false to reality, for *both–and* is more often true than *either–or.*"

APPLICATIONS

1. State the culturally conditioned moral judgment ("good" or "bad") that each of the following subjects evokes. Then explain how these

culturally conditioned attitudes are frequently compartmentalized. For example, the culturally conditioned moral judgment evoked by "honesty" is "good," "desirable." But consider this statement:

It takes two people to hurt me. An enemy to say something bad about me, and a friend to bring me the news.

In such a situation is "honesty" always a virtue?

Or consider this piece of advice from Dr. Joyce Brothers concerning honesty in marriage:

If you are unfaithful, deny it to your dying breath. [Confessing] doesn't help your marriage.

As you consider the subjects listed below, try to find *specific instances* that contradict the general culturally conditioned judgment. For example, despite *honesty*'s high repute, what do you think many people would do if they discovered, after making a purchase, that they had been undercharged?

Monogamy	Judging by appearances
Charity	Romantic love
Bribery	Drug abuse
Equality	Cheating on exams

2. According to cultural anthropologist Clyde Kluckhohn:

Cultures are like Topsy. They just grew. Once, however, a way of handling a situation becomes institutionalized, there is ordinarily great resistance to change or deviation. . . . Certain cultural premises may become totally out of accord with a new factual situation [yet] emotional loyalty continues in the face of reason because of the intimate conditioning of early childhood.

Relate Kluckhohn's observations to this statement by Albert Einstein, made nearly *forty* years ago:

The unleashed power of the atom has changed everything except our way of thinking. Thus, we are drifting toward a catastrophe beyond conception. We shall require a substantially new manner of thinking if mankind is to survive.

3. Explain the "message" of each of the following cartoons in terms of cultural conditioning.

Cobb Weekly Editorial Cartoon 286. Reprinted with permission, Sawyer Press, Los Angeles, California 90046 U.S.A.

Spectator, Bloomington, Indiana. March 11, 1969.

"You're a disgrace to all lemmings!"

Drawing by Chas. Adams; © 1974 The New Yorker Magazine, Inc.

2

Resistance to Change

The only person who likes change
is a wet baby.

ROY Z. M. BLITZER

The first man to carry an umbrella in London was attacked by an outraged mob. The first American woman to wear a one-piece bathing suit on a public beach was arrested for indecency. In 1847, Dr. Semmelweiss discovered that puerperal fever was carried from one woman to another on the unwashed hands of attending physicians. His "new idea" so outraged his medical colleagues that he was banned from practicing in the hospital where he had made the discovery, and for another fifty years, thousands of new mothers died needlessly each year. Charles Darwin's theory of natural selection was found so repugnant that, almost seventy-five years after it was first propounded, schoolteachers in Tennessee were forbidden to discuss it in the classroom. When Alexander Graham Bell first tried to get financial backing for his invention, the telephone, he was arrested and charged with attempting to obtain money under false pretenses. A local newspaper editorialized:

> He [Alexander Graham Bell] claimed he was promoting a device whereby one person could talk to another several miles away, by means of a small apparatus and some wire. Without doubt this man is a fraud and an unscrupulous trickster and must be taught that the American public is too smart to be the victim of this and similar schemes. Even if this insane idea worked it would have no practical value other than for circus sideshows.[3]

So it's gone, and so it goes: The urge to strangle the infant idea burns in the breast of all of us. New ideas and behaviors are accepted only grudgingly—tenaciously and self-righteously resisted by the masses.

And not just new ideas in the sense of "original" or "previously

44

Reprinted with special permission of King Features Syndicate, Inc.

unheard of." Also new in the sense of "new to me," "different from what I already believe."

What lies behind this seemingly innate resistance to change, this almost automatic hostility toward the new or different? Before we attempt an answer, let's go back in time.

Did you ever, as a young child, wake up in the middle of the night, in the dark, terrified and crying, just in time to save yourself from falling from a high ledge to rocks a hundred feet below? Did you ever lie rigid in your bed, awakened by some strange ominous sound, and dare not rise to turn on the light for fear the lurking beast would get you? Did you ever, when you went to bed at night, after turning off the light, jump into the bed from several feet away to escape the grasping paw of some sinister creature crouched beneath your bed, waiting to grab your leg when you approached? Did you ever, when you had gone out after dark, run for your life, trying in terror to reach the door of your home before the shadowy monster chasing you caught up and jumped you from behind, not daring to look back over your shoulder for fear of what you would see and managing to reach your home and slam the door behind you just as the unseen pursuing fiend, its panting breath hot on the back of your neck, was reaching forward to grab you?

"Yes," you may acknowledge, "I had my share of childhood nightmares and fears, like everybody else. So what?"

Reflect for a moment, if you will, on what made those nightmares and fantasies so scary. That scariness came from a terrible and terrifying sense of *threat,* a sense of threat created by the monster, witch, or beast pursuing you, or from some frightening situation such as being trapped

"No, I would not welcome a contrasting point of view."
Drawing by Bernard Schoenbaum; © 1985 The New Yorker Magazine, Inc.

in a flaming house or falling over a high cliff. So, you don't even have to accept a "deeper" psychological interpretation to agree that feeling threatened is, to say the least, extremely unpleasant.

Nevertheless, a psychoanalytic explanation of nightmares can take us one very important step further. Freudian psychologists, and many psychologists of other schools as well, believe that nightmares are caused by repressed thoughts and emotions threatening to force their way into conscious awareness. These "new ideas" ("new" because repressed and denied by our conscious mind) are so threatening to our sense of who and what we are that we become terrified. Hence, the nightmare. The nightmare serves to wake us up, so our consciousness can repress the unacceptable idea or impulse.

What's the point? Simply this: New ideas, different ideas, ideas that conflict with our conscious self-image, with our preconceptions, and with our value system—such ideas are threatening. As adults, just as when we were children, we tend to deal with the threat such ideas pose by *rejecting* them out of hand. Needless to say, the more aware of this tendency we can become, the more readily we will be able to maintain an open mind and examine new ideas objectively and dispassionately.

ETHNOCENTRISM

Ethnocentrism is just a fancy word for "mine is better"—*my* ideas, *my* values, *my* race, *my* country. Ethnocentrism serves useful and important purposes, for it lets people feel good about themselves, their group, and their country. But ethnocentrism also fosters an irrational resistance to new ideas. After all, by definition, "new" and "different" suggest *not mine, someone else's.*

THE MOTHER HEN SYNDROME

There is no easier way to make yourself hated than to criticize people's children, because people often feel that you are indirectly telling them that *they* are inferior. After all, a high-quality, valuable chicken lays high-quality, valuable eggs, and if the eggs are flawed there's obviously something wrong with the chicken. Most of us tend to feel that if our views and opinions are challenged, our value or worth as a person is at stake. We tend to perceive our ideas and opinions as the "children" of our minds. And we tend to feel just as threatened and defensive when our opinions are criticized as parents feel when someone criticizes their "actual" children, their offspring.

In cultivating the ability to reason logically, one of the most important steps of all is to train yourself not to react to ideas opposed to your own as though you were a mother hen whose eggs were being scornfully rejected.

The *accuracy* and *verifiability* of any given opinion that you may hold has nothing to do with your worth and value as a human being. If you can force yourself to accept this fact, you will have freed yourself from that chain that binds so many people, for their entire lives, to virtually every inaccurate, uninformed, and unverifiable prejudice that they picked up in their youth and young adulthood.

Ralph Waldo Emerson, the nineteenth-century American philosopher, noted that "A foolish consistency is the hobgoblin of little minds." In other words, it is the insecure, self-doubting person who feels that, having once formed an opinion about a subject, it is a sign of weakness or stupidity to change that opinion in the light of new facts, new knowledge. The larger mind says, "Do I contradict myself? Very well then, I contradict myself," because such a mind recognizes that to relinquish falsehood for truth is infinitely preferable to clinging stubbornly to ill-informed preconceptions.

FACTS, OPINIONS, AND PREJUDICES

People have a tendency to make a distinction, usually not even a conscious one, between subjects on which they feel there is only one correct opinion and subjects on which they feel there are numerous accurate opinions. They usually call the former type of opinion a "fact." By this they mean that there is such overwhelming evidence of the accuracy of the opinion that no other opinion can be held by a reasonable person. Concerning the second type of subject, a subject on which they feel that more than one opinion may be reasonably held, their attitude might be described as follows:

> It's a democracy, ain't it? So, my opinion is just as good as your opinion. (And if you don't like it, let's step outside, and I'll show you whose opinion is right!)

Making this false distinction between two types of subjects is what allows people to retain their prejudices even when confronted with evidence that to an objective observer clearly discredits their view.

To take an obvious example: It is a widely held opinion today that the earth is spherical. Most people regard this opinion as a "fact" because it can be verified, or shown to be true, by appeal to such evidence as around-the-world voyages, photographs made from satellites, and scientific principles. Similarly, the opinions that man is mortal, that if you jump off a ten-story building you will fall, that lightning is an electrical discharge and not a thunderbolt hurled by Zeus are regarded as "facts" because of the evidence that can be amassed to verify them and prove them accurate.

But all this agreement ends when we come to such controversial and in many ways more complex subjects as crime, censorship, religion, minority rights, abortion, and so forth. Here is where those blocks to logical thinking that we discussed in the first part of Section Two come into play; here is where the danger signals start flashing.

Asked to respond to subjects such as these, people often react in one of two ways, both of which are illogical.

The first way we've already discussed. They react by stating their opinion and maintaining that it's at least as valid as any other opinion. They make the false distinction between *fact* and *opinion* that we mentioned earlier and hold that, because whatever one believes on the subject is "just an opinion" (that is, not a fact, not something that can be "proven"), their opinion is as "good" (meaning as "accurate") as any other.

A second way of reacting, however, is more common and leads to even more unfortunate results. People state as their *opinion* a view that is really a *prejudice*, while actually regarding it as a *fact!*

This is getting a bit complex, so let's take a hypothetical example. Remember, what we want to show here is how a person, reacting to a controversial subject, states what he calls his *opinion* on the subject. Actually, though, his view is a *prejudice* because he is uninformed—in other words, ignorant of the subject. But although he calls his view an *opinion,* he really regards his view as a *fact* (and hence indisputable).

C. S. ROTT AND M. ATBAR

TIME: *Thursday,* 10:30 P.M.

PLACE: *The Rathskeller Bar.*

SETTING AND ATMOSPHERE: *A single long shoe-box-shaped room. Red and blue spotlights vainly try to penetrate the smog of cigarette smoke. An electric band on a platform halfway along one side of the room blares at full volume.* C. S. ROTT *fights his way toward the bar at the back end of the shoe box through scores of milling students.*

C. S. ROTT (*grabbing his stomach*): Ugh!

VOICE (*presumably belonging to the elbow jabbed in his gut*): Oops.

C. S. ROTT (*wiping beer from the back of his neck*): Damn!

VOICE (*presumably belonging to the hand holding aloft a tilted beer mug*): Hey! Watch it!

C. S. ROTT (*removing his toe from beneath the heel of someone's shoe*): Ahh!

VOICE (*presumably belonging to the heel*): Sorry.

C. S. ROTT (*squeezing his way onto the only empty barstool, which is between a student and M. Atbar—a Man at the Bar—who has obviously had a few too many*): A schooner.

BARTENDER (*who looks like he may have enough fuzz in two or three years to justify shaving once a week*): Let's see your I.D.

C. S. ROTT (*shoving it across the bar*): Here.

BARTENDER (*staring from the I.D. to* ROTT): You don't look that old to me. Let's see your driver's license.

C. S. ROTT (*shoving it across the bar*): Here.

BARTENDER (*comparing the I.D. and the driver's license*): It says here you weigh one hundred sixty, but the driver's license says one hundred fifty-five.

C. S. ROTT: I went on a diet.

BARTENDER (*dropping the cards in a puddle of stale beer*): Bourbon and water, huh?

C. S. ROTT (*wiping the cards on his pants*): A schooner.

M. ATBAR (*turning his bleary eyes on* ROTT): Even'n' son.

C. S. ROTT (*to himself*): Oh, God.

M. ATBAR: What do you think about this latest outrage the Communists are trying to pull on us?

C. S. ROTT (*shrugging hopelessly*): Uh.

M. ATBAR (*firmly*): Communism has got to be stopped somewhere.

C. S. ROTT (*automatically*): Do you mean "communism" as a political system, as a social system, or as an economic system?

M. ATBAR (*indignantly*): I mean the worldwide Communist conspiracy. It's got to be stopped.

C. S. ROTT: Well, there's Russian communism, Chinese communism, Algerian communism, East German communism, Cuban communism, Yugoslavian communism, Czechoslovakian communism . . .

M. ATBAR (*banging his fist on the bar*): I mean *Communism!* The worldwide Communist conspiracy!

C. S. ROTT: There's Trotskyite communism, Stalinist communism, revisionist communism . . .

M. ATBAR: Look! Khrushchev said, "We will bury you." We've got to stop them.

C. S. ROTT: Who's "them"?

M. ATBAR: The Communists, before they bury us.

C. S. ROTT: Khrushchev was using a metaphor.

M. ATBAR: Huh?

C. S. ROTT: He was predicting that Russia would become economically superior to the United States and achieve economic victory over her.

M. ATBAR (*angrily*): Who says? He meant what he said. That the worldwide Communist conspiracy would conquer the United States and bury it in a pile of rubble.

C. S. ROTT: But there is no worldwide Communist conspiracy. There are almost as many types of communism as there are communist nations. And . . .

M. ATBAR (*staring at* ROTT): What are you? Some sort of pinko? Some sort of Commie sympathizer?

C. S. ROTT: No.

M. ATBAR: Then what kind of rot are you talking? *Everybody* knows about the international Communist conspiracy.

C. S. ROTT: "Conspiracy" means "planning or acting together secretly." How can you claim an international Communist conspiracy exists when China and Russia have a bitter border dispute, when Castro accuses Russia of compromise with the capitalists, when the Chinese board a Russian ship to make the Russian crew members accept the doctrines of Chinese communism, when Yugoslavia institutes capitalism to stimulate production, when Albania refuses to send delegates to Russia . . .

M. ATBAR: I don't know what you're talking about. A bunch of mumbo jumbo. *Everybody* knows there's an international Communist conspiracy.

C. S. ROTT (*sipping his beer*): No.

M. ATBAR: Listen. Will the sun rise tomorrow?

C. S. ROTT: Probably.

M. ATBAR: Look, son, don't try to put me on. I *know* the sun will rise tomorrow.

C. S. ROTT: You are an optimist.

M. ATBAR: Do fish swim in the ocean?

C. S. ROTT: Yes.

M. ATBAR: Do birds fly in the sky?

C. S. ROTT: Yes.

M. ATBAR: Good. You admit the facts. Then why don't you admit that we've got to stop the international Communist conspiracy?

C. S. ROTT: Because you haven't given any evidence that there is such a thing as the international Communist conspiracy.

M. ATBAR (*jumping up and waving his fist in front of* ROTT's *face*): *Everybody* knows about the international Communist conspiracy! It's a *fact!*

C. S. ROTT (*calmly*): The fact is that you are uninformed.

M. ATBAR: Oh yeah! I'll show you who's uninformed!

(M. ATBAR *swings wildly at* C. S. ROTT. C. S. *ducks and* M. ATBAR's *fist smashes into the face of the student sitting next to* C. S. *Barstools crash! Glasses smash! Someone screams! Students climb gleefully onto tables and throw beer mugs into the melee while yelling happily, "Fight! Fight!"*

(C. S. ROTT, *clutching his drink, crawls carefully on his hands and knees until he is out of the brawl. He finds an empty table and sits down.*)
    "Rot," he says.

EVIDENCE

To return, we recall that M. Atbar's last semirational remarks were to the effect that the international Communist conspiracy was a *fact*.

No. The fact is that some people in the United States believe in the existence of an international Communist conspiracy. But a belief in the existence of something, however widespread, is not proof of its existence and is no substitute for evidence of its existence. If it were, then the insane would be possessed by demons, and lightning would be a thunderbolt cast by an angry god.

Thinking back over this scene, we can see that M. Atbar has what he claims to be an *opinion*—namely, that there exists a worldwide, monolithic Communist conspiracy to destroy the United States.

If this opinion is to be accurate and verifiable, M. Atbar must be able to show *at least* the following assertions to be true:

1. Communism is indivisible—that is, it cannot be broken down into an economic system, a political system, a social system, and so forth.
2. The various Communist nations are not divided among themselves as to the aims, means of implementation, or meaning of communism.
3. All the Communist nations have the same goal, and they are planning together in secret to achieve that goal.
4. This goal, held by all Communist nations, is the physical destruction of the United States.

However, as we have seen, M. Atbar is *uninformed*. He knows little, if anything, of the various points of view (economic, political, social, etc.) from which communism may be regarded; and he is not aware of the various forms that communism takes in different countries. Thus, M. Atbar's "opinion" that there is an international Communist conspiracy is really a *prejudice*. It is both uninformed and defended with irrational passion.

Finally, as the last part of the dialogue makes clear, M. Atbar does not really believe at all that his view that there is an international Communist conspiracy is subject to question, for he actually believes that the existence of such a conspiracy is a *fact* as self-evident as the "fact" that birds fly in the sky and fish swim in the ocean and hence requires no supporting evidence.

But the difference is that M. Atbar can *verify* the *accuracy* of his opinion that birds fly in the sky, and so forth, by citing *evidence*, either the evidence of personal experience or the evidence of authority:

1. He can speak from his personal experience.
2. He can appeal to the personal experience of C. S. Rott.
3. He can (probably after sobering up) direct C. S. Rott to sources in the public library to support his opinion.

However, he is *ignorant* on the subject of communism and cannot cite acceptable evidence to support his opinion. The best he could manage would be a vague "They say" or "Everybody knows." But ignorance added to ignorance does not add up to knowledge.

In order to arrive at an *accurate* and *verifiable* opinion on such complex and controversial subjects as we have mentioned, you must first of all:

1. Recognize your ignorance.

Believe me, this is the hardest step to take. Once it is taken, the rest is relatively easy. The next three steps are to:

2. Achieve an open mind (avoid hasty moral judgment and be objective).
3. Doubt your preconceptions (beware of primary certitude).
4. Inform yourself.

Your opinion, in other words, will be formed *after* you have informed yourself, *not before,* and it will be an informed opinion, one that you can verify and show to be accurate by citing qualified authority for your view.

NOTE: One word of warning here. There is always plenty of money to be made and power to be gained by playing on the prejudices of large groups of people. When a large number of people hate and fear a minority race or religion, you will always find charlatans who will give "reasons" for hating and fearing the group. When a murderer is loose, there's money to be made selling locks. When a population needs a scapegoat to blame for its own frustration, there's money to be made selling imaginary witches. So, when you *inform yourself,* don't turn to the panders for prejudice any more than you would turn to a quack to learn the cure for a disease. Be sure that the writers whose articles or books you read are *authorities* on the subject they are writing about. Not just authorities on something, but authorities on the subject they are discussing.

And as you read what they have to say, be alert for the appearance of any of the blocks to logical thinking we have examined. If you find several of these blocks in a given essay, you have no choice but to reject the essay, no matter how great an authority on the subject the author may be.

THE DANGER SIGNALS OF IRRATIONAL THOUGHT

You can train yourself to recognize both threat-induced and ethnocentric reactions by becoming aware of two danger signals. Whenever you find yourself responding to a person or proposal in one of the two ways that follow, beware. Unconscious forces are probably at work.

1. *Reaction formation*—an immediate, strong, emotional reaction against something. (This "something" may be an individual, a form of behavior, a proposition, or a concept.)
2. *Primary certitude*—an immediate, strong, emotional feeling: "I know the truth about that!"

Reaction formation is often symptomatic of a sense of threat; primary certitude is often the result of cultural conditioning and ethnocentrism. The two "cases" that follow show these irrational responses at work in real life:

Case I: Christmas Spirit

The manner in which cultural conditioning, hasty moral judgment, compartmentalization, and blind ethnocentrism combine to produce irrational thinking and behavior is illustrated by the following news story:

A family living in the South hanged an effigy of Santa Claus on their front lawn a few weeks before Christmas. It was their opinion that Santa Claus is a myth having nothing to do with the sacredness of the birth of Christ. By hanging a blow-up plastic Santa from a scaffold, with a noose around its neck, they hoped to dramatize their viewpoint.

The reaction of "Christian" neighbors to their action was less than tolerant. First the plastic Santa was stolen. They replaced it. A flower pot was thrown through their front window; they received abusive and obscene phone calls; people drove by and shouted threats to burn down their house. When interviewed by the press, angry neighbors accused the family of lacking the "Christmas spirit."

Although there is a certain grotesque humor in the neighbors' reaction to the irreverent treatment of Santa Claus, there is also a certain horror as well. The threat-shouting window-smashers are enslaved, their shackles not physical but mental. And their next target could be me, or you.

Case II: Get Tough!

A major problem in America's large cities today is "crime in the streets" —sudden, savage, and apparently senseless beatings, rapes, and murders of average people going about their business. What is the solution?

CRACK DOWN ON CRIME!
GET TOUGH WITH CRIMINALS!
INCREASE THE PENALTIES FOR CRIME!
UNLEASH THE POLICE!

Danger Signal 2 is flashing. A strong, immediate, emotional conviction that you "know the truth" about this problem. A feeling of "primary certitude."

Why "get tough"? Why increase the penalties?

The standard argument is that getting tough will deter potential criminals from breaking the law. If people know that they will receive much "pain" for a little "pleasure," they will be less likely to commit criminal acts.

Despite its apparent "common sense" logic, this argument contains an all-important implied assertion—that would-be law-breakers are rational individuals who always weigh potential pleasure against potential pain before they act.

But the briefest investigation into the field of criminology will show that no causal relation has ever been established between the severity of physical punishment (such as imprisonment) and the rate or seriousness of criminal acts.

Many people never make this investigation or try to understand the complex causes and problematical cures of criminal behavior. Instead of becoming suspicious of their opinions when Danger Signal 2 flashes, they perceive this feeling of "primary certitude" as evidence that they know the truth, that any fool knows that the way to stamp out crime is to get tough with the criminals.

You can avoid joining the ranks of these benighted people. Learn to *recognize* and *respect* the two danger signals of irrational thought when they occur in your thinking. If you do learn to recognize and respect them, you will be able to stop short, analyze the motivations behind your irrational reaction, force yourself to suspend hasty moral judgment, avoid either–or thinking, and achieve objectivity. And having done so, you will be in a position to think logically and rationally about the subject at hand. You will be able to analyze it as an intelligent, thoughtful person rather than merely *reacting* to it with about as much intelligence as the rat in the experimental psychologist's cage displays when it runs mindlessly to the feed trough at the flashing of a light.

IRONY

It has been said that one of the surest tests of intelligence and sophistication is the ability to recognize irony. The perception of irony always necessitates suspension of moral judgment, intellectual detachment (objectivity), and recognition of the various points of view from which a subject may be regarded. Thus, you should cultivate your ability to recognize irony as a means of cultivating your ability to think logically. Irony always involves incongruity or contrast. This contrast may take many forms: contrast between what appears to be and what is, contrast between what is intended and what is achieved, contrast between what is said and what is meant, contrast between what is and what should be.

Both cases that we have examined in this chapter reveal numerous ironies. In Case I the ironies are particularly glaring. In the name of upholding and preserving the "Christmas spirit," the abusive neighbors displayed anti-Christmas and anti-Christian behavior. In Case II there is irony of appearance–reality and of intention–achievement; the reasons people give for advocating stricter punishment of criminals are often not the real reasons why they desire stricter punishment, and punishment intended to reform criminals frequently leads to their becoming hardened in their criminal attitudes.

Frequently, the recognition of irony takes you right to the central fallacy in a particular argument:

Argument: Censorship is necessary to prevent moral corruption.

Scene: Censor watching a possibly "pornographic" movie prior to its release to the public.

Censor: Boy! Was that scene morally corrupting! Run it through again, Jack, while I'm writing up the demand that it be deleted to protect the public.

Irony: If viewing "pornography" is morally corrupting, then censors (who view such material frequently) must be more morally corrupt than the rest of us. Should we allow such degenerates to dictate our morals?

HIGHLIGHTS

- The urge to strangle the infant idea burns in the breast of all of us.

- Most of us tend to feel that if our views and opinions are challenged, our value or worth as a person is at stake.

- Reaction formation is often symptomatic of a sense of threat; primary certitude is often the result of cultural conditioning and ethnocentrism.

- Belief in the existence of something, however widespread, is not proof of its existence and is no substitute for evidence of its existence.

- One of the surest tests of intelligence and sophistication is the ability to recognize irony.

ROCK AND HILLARY
THE TALE OF A BLIND DATE GONE WRONG

If there's a whipping boy in this book, he is surely our stereotyped "dumb jock," Rock Normal, whom we've already met sponging ideas off Yvonne. But Rock does have a certain pedagogic utility. In the dialogue that follows, Rock reveals the essential dynamics of "resistance to change": ethnocentrism, primary certitude, reaction formation, and compartmentalization.

When we focus in on Rock, it's a little after nine o'clock on Friday night. He has just burst through the door of his apartment, startling his roommate, who is slaving over a term paper due on Monday. The roommate watches in puzzlement as Rock strides angrily through the living room into the kitchen, where he pours himself a stiff drink, all the while muttering curses under his breath.

ROOMMATE: What's going on? I thought you had a date.

ROCK (*returning to the living room, the drink already half drained*): I'm gonna kill Karen. Wring her neck!

ROOMMATE: Karen. Oh yeah. She's the one who fixed you up with the blind date for tonight. Let's see . . . what was her name?

ROCK (*explosively*): Hillary. Hillary Gale. What kind of name is that for a girl, anyway? Sounds like a blizzard on a mountain.

ROOMMATE (*mildly*): I take it you and she didn't exactly hit it off.

ROCK (*shaking his head incredulously*): You know what she was wearing? A *suit*, for cripes sake. With a jacket. And a tie. A *tie*, no less.

ROOMMATE: No kidding.

ROCK: That was just for openers. Not only was she dressed like a man, but she *acted* like a man. When I tried to open the car door for her, she walked around and started to get in on the other side. Said she assumed I wanted her to drive.

ROOMMATE (*smiling*): No kidding.

ROCK (*grimly*): We get to the restaurant. I ask her what she wants me to order for her. No dice. She's got to make some sort of stupid point by giving the waitress her order herself.

ROOMMATE: What's wrong with that?

ROCK (*indignantly*): A lady is supposed to let the man order. That's the way it's done.

ROOMMATE: Oh.

ROCK: So then I try to make conversation, see. Like asking her what she's studying to be. You know what she says?

ROOMMATE: Not a clue.

ROCK: A *veterinarian!* A woman, thinking she's gonna be able to be a veterinarian. Can you beat that? Anybody with an ounce of sense knows that's a man's job. I mean, she can't weigh more than a hundred and ten. How does she think she's gonna hang on to a half-ton heifer?

ROOMMATE: Beats me.

ROCK: So I try to knock a little sense into her head. After all, a woman's place is in the home.

ROOMMATE: Any luck?

ROCK (*throwing back another slug of whiskey*): How do you talk sense to someone who keeps staring two inches above the top of your head?

ROOMMATE: Come again.

ROCK: Get this. She said she was reading my "aura," whatever the hell that's supposed to be.

ROOMMATE: What did it say? Your aura?

ROCK: She started to tell me, but I cut her off. I told her anybody who believed in that sort of hocus-pocus belonged in a loony bin.

ROOMMATE: Oh.

ROCK: Listen. You haven't heard the worst part. We get the bill, see, and I pick it up like a guy's supposed to do. But she insists on looking at it, too.

ROOMMATE: So?

ROCK (*draining his drink, flushing at the memory*): So right there—I mean right *there*, with people all around us—she opens her purse and takes out her wallet and starts handing me money for her meal across the table. I mean, right up front, where everybody could *see*. I've never been so embarrassed in my life!

ROOMMATE: Is that when you decided to cut it short?

ROCK (*nodding vigorously*): That was it. The final straw. I mean, when I go on a date, I expect a woman to act like a woman.

ROOMMATE (*nodding sagely*): You had a rough one, ole buddy.

ROCK (*staring fixedly at the calendar on the wall, as though confounded*): Well I'll be damned. I just realized something.

ROOMMATE (*following Rock's gaze to the calendar*): What?

ROCK: Why the whole thing was such a bummer.

ROOMMATE: Why?

ROCK (*gesturing at the calendar with his empty glass*): Look. Today's the thirteenth. Friday the thirteenth.

APPLICATIONS: RESISTANCE TO CHANGE

1. In the dialogue "Rock and Hillary" identify statements by Rock that illustrate:
   a. ethnocentrism 47
   b. primary certitude 54
   c. reaction formation
   d. compartmentalization 37

2. Below is a list of proposed social changes that have been seriously advocated by various groups and individuals in recent years. Which of these proposed changes do you strongly favor, and which do you strongly oppose?

   Try to account for your strong approval or opposition in terms of the concepts discussed so far in this text, including cultural conditioning, hasty moral judgment, either–or thinking, compartmentalization, intolerance of ambiguity, sense of threat, and primary certitude.

At the discretion of your instructor, choose one or more of these proposals and analyze it from the *opposite* perspective from the one you hold. In other words, take a proposal you oppose and try to discover reasonable arguments supporting it, or take a proposal you favor and try to discover sound arguments against it. The purpose of this assignment is to encourage you to recognize the complexity of the issues involved in each proposal, thereby converting emotional reaction into rational assessment.

a. Federal and state laws prohibiting child labor should be repealed.
b. Homosexual marriage should be given the same legal status as heterosexual marriage.
c. Students should have the right to drop out of school at age fourteen.
d. Men and women who have helped pay for a spouse's education should have a legal claim on the spouse's future earnings if a divorce occurs.
e. Each family in America should be restricted to ownership of a single automotive vehicle.
f. Children who believe their parents are incompetent to raise them should be able to sue for "divorce" from such parents, just as a man or woman may sue for divorce from an unsatisfactory spouse.
g. Laws prohibiting human sexual activity in public should be abolished.
h. Doctors should be legally required to perform active euthanasia on terminally ill patients who ask to die.
i. There are situations in which torture is not only permissible but also called for and morally right.
j. Students who are graduated from high school without basic skills in reading, writing, and mathematics should be able to sue the school system for negligence.

APPLICATIONS: PRECONCEIVED OPINIONS

1. *Write down* what you presently believe to be the answers to each of the following questions.

2. Then, at the discretion of your instructor, choose one of the questions as the subject for a research project.
3. After you have completed your investigation, go back and mark each of your preconceptions "accurate," "inaccurate," or "partially accurate." Which label predominates?
4. Compare your answers to the other questions with the research-based information discovered by fellow students who investigated them.
   a. What are the major causes of inflation?
   b. What kind of people sign up with computerized dating services?
   c. How can you tell an alcoholic from a social drinker?
   d. What are the psychological effects of rape?
   e. What are the major sources of income for organized crime?
   f. What are the effects of TV violence on children?
   g. What are the signs of menopause in the female or climacteric in the male?
   h. What are the long-term academic benefits of early education programs such as preschool nurseries and Head Start?
   i. In primitive hunting and gathering societies, what are the principal food sources and how are they secured?
   j. What ten jobs will be most in demand in the next decade?

3

Empty Abstractions

Words are akin to empty vessels
into which we pour meanings.
SAMUEL H. STEIN

Responsible parents . . .
If there is to be *freedom* . . .
Liberty demands . . .
The only *honorable* action . . .
Justice will be done . . .
The nature of *capitalism* . . .

Tyranny always . . .
Those who are *unfaithful* to . . .
Selfishness cannot be . . .
The goal of *communism* . . .
It is *un-American* to . . .
Only *cowardice* would . . .

Whenever you find yourself beginning statements of this sort, BE-WARE!

The italicized words are unconcretized *abstractions,* and using an abstraction without *concretizing* it (rendering it concrete) always involves a hidden assertion. This implied assertion is always the same: "————— has one and only one acceptable meaning, and that meaning is the one I am using when I make my statement."

We can illustrate the way unconcretized abstractions prevent meaningful communication by constructing a hypothetical conversation between Yvonne and a casual friend of hers, Gidget. They ran into each other in the coffee line at the student union and are now sitting at a table bringing each other up to date.

A REAL MAN

GIDGET (*gushing*): Do you realize I haven't seen you since before you got married? That was months ago, wasn't it?

YVONNE: Seven.

GIDGET (*eyeing Yvonne's obviously pregnant figure*): Seven months, and just look at you—expecting already. That fellow you married, Sott . . .

YVONNE: Rott, C. S. Rott.

GIDGET: Rott, that's right. He must be a *real man!*

YVONNE (*mildly*): Yes, I think C. S. is a real man.

GIDGET (*thrusting her left hand under Yvonne's nose*): Look! I'm engaged!

YVONNE: That's nice. What's he like?

GIDGET (*ecstatically*): Tony? Oh, he's a *real man!* You'll see, he's supposed to meet me here.

YVONNE: When are you planning . . .

GIDGET (*interrupting excitedly*): Look! There he is now! (*She waves and cries out, "Tony! Over here!"*)

(*Yvonne turns in her chair and sees Tony bulldozing his way toward their table. A slightly built male student carrying a cup of coffee gets indifferently knocked out of Tony's path. He starts to protest but thinks better of it when Tony grabs him by his coffee-stained shirt and bellows loud enough for the whole cafeteria to hear, "Bug off, creep!"*)

GIDGET (*beaming with pride*): See what I mean? A *real man.*

TONY (*approaching their table*): Hi ya, girls! (*Yvonne starts to say "hello" but gags on the thick blanket of stale sweat that settles over the table.*)

GIDGET (*standing and running her hand caressingly through the matted black fur that protrudes from the top of Tony's T-shirt*): Been weight lifting?

TONY (*flexing the bulging biceps of his right arm appraisingly*): Yeah. (*He flips a chair around and sits with his arms folded over the back rest. He glances at Yvonne*): Who knocked you up, baby?

GIDGET: This is Yvonne. She's married to C. S. Rott.

TONY (*indifferently*): Rott, huh. How much can he bench press?

YVONNE: What?

GIDGET: Lift. Tony means how much weight can C. S. lift in a bench press.

YVONNE: I really don't know.

TONY (*standing up and speaking to Gidget*): Time to break up the ole hen party. Some of the boys are having a keggar.

GIDGET (*in a stage whisper to Yvonne*): What did I tell you? He's a *real man,* isn't he?

TONY (*over his shoulder as he starts to walk away*): Move it!

GIDGET (*hastily to Yvonne, as she rises*): Bye!

YVONNE: Bye. (*Tony and Gidget depart. After a few minutes C. S., who has just gone through the lunch line, comes to the table.*)

C. S.: Hi. What happened to the people I saw you with when I came in?

YVONNE: They left.

C. S.: Who were they?

YVONNE: A girl I used to know and her fiancé, a guy named Tony.

C. S.: He looked like a hairy ape. What's he like?

YVONNE (*decisively*): He's a *real ass.*

The point, needless to say, is that one woman's real man is another's obnoxious slob. The term "real man" is an abstraction, not an absolute. And, as such, it may have quite different meanings to different people. It is not a term with a concrete, universally agreed upon denotation, such as "door" or "sewing machine."

Unconcretized abstractions are inherently vague and ambiguous, which is why their use in writing and discourse prevents accurate communication and often blocks logical thinking. An abstract term, when left unconcretized, also tends to obscure the complexity of a subject. One gets the impression that there is a single agreed-upon "definition" of the term, when in fact there may be numerous "definitions," some of which are quite incompatible.

If Tony had not come along and, through his speech and behavior, concretized what Gidget meant by "real man," Yvonne might not have realized that she and Gidget profoundly *disagreed* about those qualities that constitute manliness.

This is the heart of the matter. The use of empty abstractions often creates *apparent agreement* where there is *no agreement at all.* The use of unconcretized abstract terms prevents what is really being talked about from becoming apparent.

We must get a firm grasp of the nature of abstract terms if we are to avoid the many pitfalls they pose. So let's examine the matter a little further.

So far, we have seen that unconcretized abstract terms:

1. Apparently have a fixed and definite meaning (denotation), but really don't
2. Are actually vague and ambiguous
3. Obscure the complexity of a subject
4. Tend to create apparent agreement where there may be no agreement at all.

If you will recall the sampling of abstract terms at the beginning of this chapter, you will perceive that abstract terms tend to have two other characteristics that also block logical thinking. They often:

5. Contain a built-in *moral judgment*
6. Encourage *either–or thinking.*

As culturally conditioned twentieth-century Americans, we tend to react to the italicized abstractions in the left-hand column on page 62 as "good," "right," "desirable," and to react to those in the right-hand column as "bad," "wrong," "undesirable."

These six characteristics of abstract terms that we have listed make them *very* powerful tools in the hands of people who wish to influence us. These people may have what they consider our best interests at heart, or they may be trying to gain control over us for their own ends. Whatever their motive, it is important that we, as citizens of a democracy in a complex age requiring intelligent decisions, should not become the mindless puppets of skillful orators and writers who want to manipulate us.

A famous passage in Ernest Hemingway's novel *A Farewell to Arms* describes how politicians used unconcretized abstractions during World War I in order to justify the war and to rationalize a continuation of the slaughter. Frederick, an American volunteer, mentions the possibility of losing the war; Gino, an Italian patriot, responds:

> "We won't talk about losing. There is enough talk about losing. What has been done this summer [an unsuccessful offensive costing tens of thousands of lives] cannot have been done in vain."
>
> I did not say anything. I was always embarrassed by the words *sacred, glorious* and *sacrifice* and the expression *in vain*. We had heard them, sometimes standing in the rain almost out of earshot, so that only the shouted words came through, and had read them, on proclamations that were slapped up by billposters over other proclamations, now for a long time, and I had seen nothing sacred and the things that were glorious had no glory and the sacrifices were like the stockyards at Chicago if nothing was done with the meat except to bury it. . . .[4]

IN GOD'S NAME

It has been said that the greatest sins in humanity's history have been committed in the name of God. What is meant by this apparently irreverent assertion is that, when a reprehensible or unwise action is contemplated, an action for which *logical arguments* would be hard to find, the action can often be made to seem good by committing it *in the name of* an abstraction considered "sacred."

In other words, one way to prevent logical, rational analysis of an action, a law, or a policy is to take that action, pass the law, or form the policy in the name of some abstraction considered unquestionably "good" or in the name of opposition to some abstraction considered unquestionably "bad."

Thus, if a nation is following a certain policy, leaders may attempt (whether in good or bad faith) to win support for the policy and stifle criticism of it by claiming that the nation's "honor" is at stake. To oppose the policy becomes, then, to want the nation to "betray its honor" or behave "dishonorably." Those who exercise intelligence will perceive that "honor" is an abstraction, not a thing. Hence, to suggest that people who oppose a policy want the nation to act dishonorably is a way of preventing a rational, logical analysis of the merits of the policy.

DENOTATION AND CONNOTATION

Abstractions derive much of their power from our feeling that words stand for things—that words point to specific objects or acts. Some do: "cat," "car," "house," "run," and "hike," for example. The specific object or act that a word points to is called the word's *denotation.* Other words have *no fixed denotation.* Abstractions are words of this type. However, an abstraction does tend to have a fixed and definite *connotation.* The connotation of an abstraction is the emotional reaction it evokes. This connotation can generally be described as "good," "neutral," or "bad."

Denotation is *outer.* It's what a word or expression points to.

Connotation is *inner.* It's your reaction (favorable, neutral, negative) to a word or expression.

Often, as the Peanuts cartoon illustrates, the *only* difference between two abstract words is their connotation.

This characteristic of the unconcretized abstract term, its lack of a fixed, specific denotation, is what makes its use in composition (and in any other context) so undesirable. There is the illusion of meaning, perhaps even of profundity, when actually there may be no meaning at all:

HOUSTON (AP)—The parent of a Houston high school pupil received a message from the principal about a special meeting on a proposed educational program.

It read:

"Our school's cross-graded, multi-ethnic, individualized learning program is designed to enhance the concept of an open-ended learning program with emphasis on a continuum of multi-ethnic, academically enriched learn-

© 1966 *United Feature Syndicate, Inc.*

ing using the identified intellectually gifted child as the agent or director of his own learning.

"Major emphasis is on cross-graded, multi-ethnic learning with the main objective being to learn respect for the uniqueness of a person."

The parent wrote the principal:

"I have a college degree, speak two foreign languages and four Indian dialects, have been to a number of county fairs and three goat ropings, but I haven't the faintest idea as to what the hell you are talking about. Do you?"

A character in a play, admonished to think before speaking, responded to this effect: "But how can I know what I think till I hear what I say?" This is rather amusing. Considerably less amusing, however, is the fact that many people don't know what they mean even *after* they've said what they think.

Yvonne's father, whom you are going to meet in the dialogue that follows, is a person of this sort.

C. S. Rott and Yvonne's Father

The setting is the home of Yvonne's parents, where C. S. Rott and Yvonne are visiting. C. S. and Yvonne's father are sitting in the living room, facing each other across a sea of carpet. Yvonne's mother has made an excuse to take Yvonne to another part of the house, so C. S. and his father-in-law can talk "man to man."

Yvonne's father is skimming through the evening newspaper, a daily masochistic ritual punctuated by derisive snorts of outrage and embittered self-righteousness. Suddenly, he flings a section of the paper at C. S.

YVONNE'S FATHER: Look at that, will you! (*C. S. picks up the paper and tries to make out what Yvonne's father wants him to take a look at.*)

C. S. ROTT (*cautiously*): Uh . . . What?

YVONNE'S FATHER: The story about the dame. (*C. S. makes out the item Yvonne's father is referring to. It concerns a female secretary who was fired for refusing to fetch coffee for an all-male office staff and who filed a lawsuit to regain her job.*)

YVONNE'S FATHER (*who has been watching C. S.*): You finished reading it?

C. S. ROTT: Yes.

YVONNE'S FATHER: I hope she loses.

C. S. ROTT: Why?

YVONNE'S FATHER (*getting more and more worked up as he talks*): Kooks like that don't deserve to have a job. Can you imagine anything more unreasonable? Any normal woman would be happy to go get coffee.

Apparently Yvonne's father has actually said something. Apparently he has said what he thinks about the woman. Apparently he has communicated his opinions to C. S.

Actually, he has communicated nothing except an attitude, a hasty moral judgment. He has said nothing.

C. S. wants to pin him down, but he isn't going to have much luck.

C. S. ROTT: What do you mean when you say she's "unreasonable"?

YVONNE'S FATHER: Refusing to go get coffee is ridiculous.

C. S. ROTT: Why?

YVONNE'S FATHER: Because it's her *duty*.

C. S. ROTT: Who says?

YVONNE'S FATHER (*scornfully*): "Who says?" Nobody *says*, it just is. A secretary's supposed to be loyal and obedient, do everything she's told.

C. S. ROTT (*mildly*): Wash her employer's socks? Walk his dog?

YVONNE'S FATHER (*glaring at C. S.*): Not *everything*. Everything *reasonable!*

C. S. ROTT: You've acknowledged that a secretary shouldn't be compelled to do things irrelevant to her job. Isn't fetching coffee irrelevant?

YVONNE'S FATHER (*striking the arm of his chair with his fist*): They're not the same at all! Demanding that she wash socks or walk a dog is *unreasonable;* telling her to go for coffee is *reasonable!* If you can't understand that, then you're as stupid as that secretary! What kind of idiot has my daughter married?

YVONNE (*rushing into the living room*): Daddy! C. S.! Please!

CONCRETIZATION

Yvonne's father is unable to concretize his abstraction "unreasonable." Instead, he explains what he means by this abstraction in terms of *other* unconcretized abstractions: being *ridiculous,* not doing one's *duty,* not being *loyal* or *obedient.* When C. S. tries to get him to concretize these judgmental abstractions, Yvonne's father is unable to do so.

Like Yvonne's father, people often state their opinions on a subject *entirely* in terms of empty abstractions. If you ask them to explain their meaning, they will do so in terms of additional empty abstractions. No meaningful communication can occur, however, unless each of the abstractions is concretized. If you keep pushing such people to explain what they mean, they often become quite threatened and may become defensive and angry. This is why "argument" has acquired the unfortunate but revealing connotation of dissension and ill will.

Such people become threatened because *they really don't know what they mean.* People who cannot concretize the abstractions they are using quite literally don't know what they're talking about.

We noted earlier that the use of an unconcretized abstraction always involves an implied assertion that "———— has one and only one acceptable meaning, and that meaning is the one I am using when I make my statement." People who can't concretize the abstraction they are using *don't even know the meaning that they mean.*

Let's take the central abstraction in the dialogue between Yvonne's father and C. S. Rott—*reasonable*—and examine it more closely. A dictionary doesn't help; when we look up the word, we find this definition:

Reasonable: agreeable or in accord with *reason* or *sound judgment; logical; sensible; intelligent; judicious; wise; equitable* (abstractions italicized).

However, we now know no more than we did before. Because *reasonable* is an abstraction, it has no single definite, concrete, universally agreed-upon signification in the world of concrete instances. Therefore, all a dictionary can do is define the word in terms of other abstractions. If we're going to use the word meaningfully, we have to do better than this.

Before we can judge whether or not the secretary's refusal to fetch coffee was "reasonable," we must formulate the word's possible meanings; we must concretize the abstraction before we can assert whether or not a given action is "reasonable."

> *Concretization 1*—"To me, it is *reasonable* to both expect and require an employee to perform whatever tasks the employer may desire, as long as such tasks do not involve criminal conduct. If an employee doesn't want to perform such tasks, he or she has the option of quitting. An employee who refuses to do what the boss says, and yet expects to be kept on, is being *unreasonable*."

> *Concretization 2*—"To me, it is *reasonable* to both expect and require an employee to perform the specific skill-related tasks in which he or she had to demonstrate competency in order to be hired. An employee should not be required to perform personal services or other tasks that are irrelevant to his or her profession or trade. It is perfectly *reasonable* for an employee to refuse to perform such irrelevant tasks, without jeopardizing his or her employment."

Presumably, the secretary who was dismissed from her job would concretize "reasonable" as in Concretization 2. If so, in her terms, she was acting reasonably when she refused to accept the menial task, irrelevant to her secretarial skills, of fetching coffee.

If Yvonne's father had been able to concretize what he meant by "reasonable," he might have come up with a statement similar to Concretization 1. Judged against such a concretization, the secretary's behavior was indeed unreasonable.

As you can see, concretizing an abstraction does not necessarily *resolve* an issue. Rather, concretizing an abstraction clarifies the nature of the issue—it makes clear what the real issue is.

Linguist Samuel H. Stein admonishes: "We must be aware that words are akin to empty vessels into which we pour meanings." Yes. And again, yes. Without concretization, an abstraction is *empty of meaning.*

In the 1950s Texas billionaire H. L. Hunt once observed, "You don't have to be rich to be happy." This pious sentiment evoked pleased smiles and nods among the audience. But then Hunt poured some meaning into his empty vessels, adding: "One or two million is enough for anybody to get by on."

EUPHEMISMS

Euphemisms are pleasant words used in place of unpleasant ones, nice words used in place of blunt words. In short, a euphemism is a word with a good (or at least neutral) connotation used in place of a word with a bad connotation.

Many euphemisms are relatively harmless, serving to protect our sensibilities: "go to the bathroom" instead of "urinate"; "custodian" instead of "janitor"; "passed away" instead of "died." But even these socially polite terms reveal an essential characteristic of all euphemisms: vagueness is substituted for specificity.

The abuse of euphemisms occurs when—as in the two accompanying cartoons—they are used as a sort of verbal magic to make the underlying reality disappear. Who could find enslavement and mass murder in "final solution"? What's become of the invading tanks and troops in "protective reaction strike"? Where's the blood and destruction in "reconnaissance in force"?

Thus, with euphemisms as with unconcretized abstractions, we must peer through the verbal smokescreen to discern the concrete reality beyond.

SUMMARY

Unconcretized abstractions subtly block logical thinking by giving an impression of meaning where little or none exists. They are sound and fury signifying nothing.

For Better or For Worse   by Lynn Johnston

Detroit *Free Press*, May 17, 1980. Copyright, 1980, Universal Press Syndicate.

Reprinted from *Church & State*, Vol. 30, No. 6, June 1977. © 1977.

Whenever you use an abstraction, ask yourself:

"Have I clearly and calmly explained what I am referring to in the
world of concrete reality by the abstraction?"

"Have I given some specific and sufficiently detailed examples of what I
mean by the term?"

If the answer to these questions is "yes," you are using the abstraction
legitimately.

The *illegitimate* use of abstractions generally occurs in the context
of other types of appeals to emotion. It usually appears in writing or
speeches characterized by lots of high-sounding words; characterized by
lots of words that are "sacred" ("motherhood," "God," "country") or
"profane" ("communism," "decay," "injustice"); and characterized by
a lack of concrete, specific, factual, and calmly presented instances. You
can easily train yourself to recognize and scorn this type of manipulative
rhetoric.

Below are reprinted two brief examples of the illegitimate use of
abstractions. And two examples of their legitimate use follow.

Illegitimate Use of Abstract Words

An informed citizenry, alert to guard our heritage, will guarantee strengthened sinews and heightened resolve that our flag on high will never be replaced with the butcher-red emblem of barbarous, godless communist slavery.[5]

Blocks to logical thinking displayed in this passage:

Abstract and undefined terms ("heritage," "barbarous," "godless," "communist," "slavery")

Implied assertion (Communism is slavery.)

Moral judgment (Communism is evil.)

Either–or thinking (Communism is all bad.)

Emotive language ("sinews," "butcher-red")

Movies are dirtier than ever.
Books are dirtier than ever.
The magazine stands are reeking.

We have come half-circle from the Victorianism of the past to the libertinism of the present. It's a little hard to see how we can get much lower . . .[6]

Blocks to logical thinking displayed in this passage:

Abstract and undefined terms ("Victorianism," "libertinism")

Moral judgment (It's "dirty" to show nudity or sexual acts.)

Either–or thinking (Victorianism versus libertinism)

Emotive language ("dirtier," "reeking," "lower")

NOTE: The various blocks to logical thinking hang together. When you eliminate one, you often find that you have eliminated several. For example, the single term "libertinism" in the second quotation above is an unconcretized abstraction, involves an implied assertion, reveals hasty moral judgment, and indicates either–or thinking. Furthermore, the writer's whole hysterical condemnation of showing the nude human body or dealing with matters of sex in movies, books, and magazines reinforces resistance to change and cultural conditioning and exploits unconscious needs and fears. (Actually, the writer may not believe one word of what he is saying but may be trying to manipulate his audience by playing on *their* culturally conditioned attitudes, *their* unconscious fears, *their* emotions. Don't let him or others like him manipulate you!)

Legitimate Use of Abstract Words

Four years ago, Carlena Gist, 26, entered a skilled-trades apprentice program at the General Motors Hydra-Matic transmission plant next to the Willow Run Airport in Ypsilanti, Michigan.

She knew it was not going to be easy. The skilled trades used to be stamped "Men Only." Even now, only about three percent of all apprentice positions in the trades are occupied by women. And Gist is the only woman machine-repair apprentice at Hydra-Matic.

The anguish, she says, began for her on day one.

There was the jealousy from the male co-workers. The taunts about being a woman in a man's job. But most of all, there was the sexual harassment.

The unwanted pinches, pats and hugs from both supervisors and co-workers. The promises of "going easy on you if you'll sleep with me" from supervisors. The repulsive, obscene catcalls. The out-loud guesses about her bust size. And the gynecological overkill of *Hustler* centerfolds and pictures of female genitalia plastered on toolboxes and held up to Carlena Gist's face.[7]

NOTE: The key abstraction in this news feature is the term "sexual harassment." In the final paragraph the reporter concretizes the abstraction by giving us numerous and specific instances.

I don't know whether history repeats itself, but biography certainly does. The other day, Michael came in and asked me what a "jerk" was—the same question Carolyn put to me a dozen years ago.

At that time, I fluffed her off with some inane answer, such as "A jerk isn't a very nice person" but both of us knew it was an unsatisfactory reply. When she went to bed, I began trying to work up a suitable definition.

It is a marvelously apt word, of course. Until it was coined, not more than 25 years ago, there was really no single word in English to describe the kind of person who is a jerk—"boob" and "simp" were too old hat, and besides they really didn't fit, for they could be lovable, and a jerk never is.

Thinking it over, I decided that a jerk is *basically a person without insight.* He is not necessarily a fool or a dope, because some extremely clever persons can be jerks. In fact, it has little to do with intelligence as we commonly think of it; it is, rather, a kind of subtle but pervasive aroma emanating from the inner part of the personality.

I know a college president who can be described only as a jerk. He is not an unintelligent man, nor unlearned, nor even unschooled in the social amenities. Yet he is a jerk *cum laude,* because of a fatal flaw in his nature —he is totally incapable of looking into the mirror of his soul and shuddering at what he sees there.

A jerk, then, is a man (or woman) who is utterly unable to see himself as he appears to others. He has no grace, he is tactless without meaning to be, he is a bore even to his best friends, he is an egotist without charm. All of us are egotists to some extent, but most of us—unlike the jerk—are perfectly and horribly aware of it when we make asses of ourselves. The jerk never knows.[8]

NOTE: The abstract term here is "jerk," and once again you will observe that the author extensively clarifies, specifies, and details what *he* means by the term. There is nothing wrong with using abstractions. Using them is necessary. But they must be concretized in a clear, calm, and objective fashion if meaningful communication is to result.

One final comment on abstractions. I have used throughout this chapter the phrase "unconcretized abstraction" to refer to a particular block to logical thinking. I have spoken of concretizing an abstraction as necessary. I have avoided stating that you should "define" an abstraction, because to do so might *erroneously* suggest that it is possible to discover and forever fix a single, universally agreed-to, "right" meaning of an abstract term. This is not possible. Only concrete words have generally agreed-upon meanings. You can consult ten randomly chosen individuals and come up with ten compatible definitions of the animal "wolf" or the object "tree."

But abstractions are different. With abstractions, *the user creates the meaning.* So the best you can do, and the most you can demand of others, is to *concretize* the abstraction. If an abstraction is concretized, you can at least determine what the user of the term means by it.

HIGHLIGHTS

- The use of empty, abstract terms often creates apparent agreement where there is really no agreement at all.
- The connotation of an abstraction is the emotional reaction it evokes. This connotation can generally be described as "good," "neutral," or "bad."
- Without concretization, an abstraction is empty of meaning.
- The abuse of euphemisms occurs when they are used as a sort of verbal magic to make the underlying reality disappear.
- With abstractions, the user creates the meaning.

APPLICATIONS

1. Often, the manner in which an abstraction is legally concretized has far-ranging implications for both society and the individual. Is a mobile home to be legally regarded as a residence or as a vehicle? The legal rights of the occupants of one and the legal rights of occupants of the other are vastly different. Is "intoxicated" to be concretized as a reading of 0.05 or 0.10 or 0.15 on a breathalyzer test? The potential consequences for the person who drinks and then drives are enormous.

Consider the four different "definitions" of *sexual harassment* printed below:

Unwelcome sexual advances shall be prohibited and shall become illegal [sexual harassment] (1) if the employee's submission is an explicit or implicit condition of employment, (2) if the employee's response becomes a basis for employment decision, or (3) if the advances interfere with the worker's performance, creating a hostile or offensive environment.

U.S. Equal Employment Opportunity Commission

Sexual harassment means (1) unsolicited, non-reciprocal, physical or verbal conduct or communication of a sexual nature, which conduct or communication is demeaning, abusive, or otherwise inappropriate; (2) a statement or implication that lack of consent to a social invitation or sexual intercourse or contact will adversely affect a person's opportunity for employment, education, public accommodation, housing, public service, membership in an organization, compensation, or the terms, conditions, or privileges of employment, education, public accommodation, housing, public service, membership in an organization or compensation.

Proposed Amendment to Michigan's Elliott-Larsen Civil Rights Act

Sexual harassment is repeated or unwarranted verbal or physical sexual advances, sexually explicit derogatory statements, or sexually discriminatory remarks made by someone in the workplace which are offensive or objectionable to the recipient or which cause the recipient discomfort or humiliation or which interfere with the recipient's job performance.

National Organization for Women (NOW) and Working Women's Institute

Sexual harassment includes (1) sexual relations, sexual contact or the threat of, or coercion for the purpose of, sexual relations or sexual contact, which is not freely and mutually agreeable to both parties; (2) the continual or repeated verbal abuse of a sexual nature, including but not limited to, graphic commentaries on the victim's body, sexually suggestive objects or pictures in the work place, sexually degrading words used to describe the victim, or propositions of a sexual nature; (3) the threat or insinuation that lack of sexual submission will adversely affect the victim's employment, wages, advancement, assigned duties or shifts, academic standing, or other conditions that affect the victim's livelihood.

Michigan Task Force on Sexual
Harassment in the Workplace

Now turn back and reread the news feature concerning Carlena Gist on page 74. Let's assume a woman experienced all the behaviors listed *except* the direct sexual propositions mentioned in the second sentence of the last paragraph.

Under which of the foregoing "definitions" would she have experienced sexual harassment?

Under which of the foregoing "definitions" would she *not* have experienced sexual harassment?

Is any one of these "definitions" the *right* definition of sexual harassment? Why or why not?

2. In the statements below, underline the abstract terms. Then:

Identify the connotation of each abstraction as positive, neutral, or negative.

Explain how the use of unconcretized abstractions in each statement tends to create apparent agreement where there may be no agreement at all and also obscures the complexity of the subject or issue.

a. "Constructive criticism is one thing; sterile negativism something else."
b. "True love is total acceptance of the loved one."
c. "Reckless abandon is not the answer to rigidity."
d. "If you're going to drink and drive, drink responsibly."
e. "Obscene material is material which deals with sex in a manner appealing to prurient interest." (Supreme Court Justice William Brennan)
f. "Every child needs discipline."
g. "End big government. Return responsibility to state and local government."
h. "A good teacher is firm, fair, and friendly."

  i. "Liberty, not license."
  j. "Nothing is more important for America than to preserve its national security."

3. Sometimes, even words that at first glance seem precise and specific actually have a high degree of vagueness, as the cartoon graphically illustrates.

   Explain how the "concrete" word italicized in each of the following sentences is actually vague and ambiguous.

   a. "I can't be drunk, officer. I've had only two *drinks.*"
   b. "No *vehicles* allowed."
   c. "Feeding national park animals is *dangerous.*"

ONE-MARTINI LUNCH

Drawing by Ziegler; © 1979 The New Yorker Magazine, Inc.

d. "Entertain your friends and neighbors with a Tupperware *party.*"

e. "We better stay in port today. I see the Coast Guard has issued a *small-craft* advisory."

4. Newspaper columnist Sidney J. Harris has satirized the way empty abstractions are often used in a self-serving and self-righteous manner. Here are a few of his "Antics with Semantics":

I am in favor of "liberty"; you are in favor of "license"; he is in favor of "anarchy."

I am "diplomatic"; you are "smooth-tongued"; he is "two-faced."

I am giving the matter "judicious consideration"; you are "overly deliberate"; he is "stalling."

I am "cautious"; you are "timid"; he is "cowardly."

I believe in "authority"; you believe in "force"; he believes in "violence."

Using Harris's "me-you-he" technique, construct five antics with semantics of your own.

5. Carefully page through a copy of today's newspaper or the latest issue of *Time* or *Newsweek,* and write down the euphemisms you find. For each instance, state bluntly and specifically the reality that the euphemism disguises.

ERRORS IN LOGICAL THINKING

Up to now we've concentrated on the major forces—cultural, psychological, and linguistic—that interfere with clear thinking. However, there are also specific reasoning errors, called "logical fallacies," that block critical thinking and often go unrecognized.

Basically, logical argument proceeds either by *induction* or by *deduction*. *Inductive* argument proceeds from specific to general, *deductive* argument from general to specific. In both types of reasoning, there are pitfalls into which the unwary may stumble.

After discussing the major fallacies of induction and deduction, we will examine a third category of faulty logic, fallacies of *relevance*.

1

Fallacies of Induction

You are already well acquainted with and adept at inductive reasoning whether or not the term itself is familiar. Anyone who has been stung by a bee or wasp has formed certain generalizations on the basis of that specific instance, one of which is "bee and wasp stings hurt" and another of which may—if you're like me—be "wave your arms and run like mad!" "Learning by experience" and "inductive reasoning" are basically the same.

But things can go wrong in this process—in logic just as in life. Many irrational childhood fears and phobias result from inductive reasoning gone haywire, generalizations reached too quickly on the basis of too few or unrepresentative instances: an encounter with a mean dog leading to a fear of all dogs, for example. In logic, we would call this a *hasty conclusion,* and adulthood confers no immunity to such fallacious reasoning.

FAULTY CAUSATION

The same longings for certainty, truth, and decisive answers that encourage either–or thinking also encourage faulty cause–effect inductive reasoning. One type of causation fallacy (*oversimplification*) alleges that a certain "effect" or phenomenon has a single cause, whereas actually there are a number of contributory causes. Another type (*post hoc ergo propter hoc:* "after this, therefore because of this") asserts that, because one event or situation occurred before a subsequent event, the later event was caused by the earlier one. Still another type of faulty causation (*hasty conclusion*) results when a conclusion is based on insufficient evidence.

You can guard against causation fallacies by always keeping two basic principles in mind:

Correlation is not causation.

Human events have multiple causes.

Correlation versus Causation

In all cause–effect relationships, there is also a *correlation* between cause and effect. When one occurs, the other occurs. They are mutually related.

The metal becomes fatigued → the wing of the plane gives way.

A man drinks ten highballs in an hour → he becomes intoxicated.

But this principle cannot be reversed. A *correlation* between two events does not *in itself* establish a causal relationship between the two. The mere fact that one event precedes or accompanies another (correlation) does not necessarily mean that it *causes* that event.

Consider the following newspaper report, based on a study published in *Pediatrics*.

TOO MUCH TV TIME CAN TURN KIDS INTO CHUBBIES

A doctor has some advice for parents of chubby children: Turn off the television set.

Heavy doses of TV make children fat, says Dr. William Deitz Jr. of the New England Medical Center. Youngsters who spend a lot of time in front of the television in their pre-teen years often become obese adolescents.

"If there is a problem of obesity in the family or if their child is becoming overweight, [parents] should consider reducing the amount of television time as a way of treating that problem," said Deitz.

He suspects that devoted TV viewers are fatter than other youngsters because they eat more and exercise less.

Deitz's study, conducted with Dr. Steven L. Gortmaker of Harvard School of Public Health, was published in the May [1985] issue of *Pediatrics*.

"What was striking to us was that compared to many of the variables that have been associated with obesity in the past—such as social class, family structure and birth order—television was just about the best predictor of obesity," Gortmaker said.

The research showed that normal-size youngsters who watched a lot of television in their pre-teen years were more likely than moderate viewers to be overweight by their teens.

Among these adolescents, the incidence of obesity increased by about two percent for each additional hour that they averaged in front of the television each day. Ten percent of the teenagers who watched an hour or less of TV a day were obese, compared with 20 percent of those who watched more than five hours daily.

The research was based on surveys conducted by the National Center for Health Statistics. Experts estimated youngsters' obesity by measuring the amount of fat in their arms. Between 1963 and 1965, they examined 6,965 children, 6–11, then surveyed 6,671 adolescents, 12–17, from 1966 to 1970. One-third of the adolescents were in both surveys.

By Daniel Haney, Associated Press, Detroit Free Press, *May 14, 1985. Used by permission of The Associated Press.*

At first glance, the headlined conclusion may appear well supported by the evidence cited. The sample of children surveyed was large, the means of evaluating and defining obesity was objective and scientific, and the credentials of the researchers are impeccable.

But look closely at the statistics on which the cause → effect generalization is based: "Ten percent of teenagers who watched an hour or less of TV a day were obese, compared with 20 percent of those who watched *more than five hours daily*" (italics added).

Let's reflect for a moment on pre-teens and teenagers who spend *more than thirty-five hours a week* peering at the TV set, month after month, year after year. Would such young people be likely to have an active social life? Would they be likely to have extensive extracurricular interests and activities? Would they be likely to be high-achieving students academically? And *why* would a young person choose to spend virtually all of his or her free time in front of the tube? Would you expect such an individual to feel good about himself or herself? To have a lot of friends? To be socially adept and popular with peers?

In short, might not both excessive TV watching and obesity result from something quite different, such as low self-esteem, socialization problems, family problems, emotional distress, academic problems, or some combination of these and other potential causes?

All the study has actually demonstrated is a *correlation* between excessive TV viewing and obesity in some teenagers. The actual cause (or, more probably, *multiple causes*) of teenage obesity may lie elsewhere, with excessive TV watching being merely a symptom rather than the cause—much less the sole cause.

Who knows? Not I. But until such *alternative possibilities* are addressed by researchers and conclusively eliminated, it would be premature to accept as proven the cause → effect relationship asserted in this report.

Whenever a cause → effect relationship is asserted, see whether it can be explained as a correlation instead.

For example, it was discovered some years ago that a higher percentage of people died of respiratory diseases in Arizona than in any other state: a fact. This finding produced a great deal of consternation. Living in Arizona *caused* lung disease—or so many people inferred. Actually, however, what had happened was this: Many people with *existing* respiratory disorders such as asthma, hay fever, bronchitis, and emphysema had moved to Arizona seeking relief from their illnesses and had remained there until they died. Correlation, yes; causation, no. The truth of the matter lay in an *alternative explanation*.

Alternative Explanation

Often, the most effective and convincing way to demonstrate faulty causation is to point out a possible *alternative explanation* for the alleged cause → effect relationship.

Bear in mind that you don't have to prove your hypothetical alternative explanation. All you have to do is show that it hasn't been ruled out as a possible cause. For only a cause → effect argument that excludes *all* alternative explanations can be regarded as conclusive.

Take this report, which claims to prove that labor strikes *cause* social and economic decline:

> Do strikes serve social progress? Strike statistics from Germany, France, England and Italy during the years 1968–73 prove they do not. The countries with the greatest number of strikes (England and Italy) showed the smallest increase in real income as well as the highest rates of inflation and currency devaluation. . . .
>
> On the other hand, the fewer the strikes, the greater the social productivity. Germany and France [had far fewer strikes and] attained the highest rates of national product growth with accompanying lower rates of inflation and increased currency values.

The report demonstrates a correlation between strikes and unhealthy economies, but does it prove a causal connection between the two? The answer is "No," because there are possible alternative explanations for the high rate of strikes in England and Italy and the low rate in Germany and France.

For example, could it not be that strikes are a *result* of economic decline rather than the sole cause of such decline? Is it not plausible that workers in a booming economy with low inflation and increasing currency values would have little reason to strike, whereas workers in countries where wages were being eroded by high inflation and declining currency values would have strong incentives to strike? Maybe yes, maybe no. But until such alternative explanations are addressed and ruled out, the cause → effect relationship alleged has not been proven.

Even quite sophisticated researchers sometimes mistake a correlation for causation. A well-known case in point occurred during a productivity experiment at a Western Electric plant in Hawthorne, Illinois. The efficiency experts hired by the company noted that the lighting in the plant was below par and theorized that, with brighter illumination of the work area, productivity might rise. So they installed brighter lights and, sure enough, productivity rose. They made the lights still brighter; productivity rose again. Clear-cut cause and effect, right? Wrong.

Shortly after the efficiency experts departed, a curious thing happened. Worker productivity in the plant declined right back to where it had been before all the expensive bright new lights were installed.

Management was confounded. Back came the experts. This time, someone suggested *dimming* the lights. The lights were dimmed; productivity rose. The lights were dimmed more, and still more, until eventually the level of illumination approximated moonlight. And yet productivity remained far higher than usual. Weird.

Finally, it dawned on the experts that the rise and fall of worker productivity had nothing at all to do with the lighting; it had to do with the presence of the efficiency experts themselves. When they were around, the workers felt more important, they got more attention, their improved performance was noticed and praised. It was the presence and social behavior of the researchers, not their fiddling with the lights, that caused productivity to rise. (The town where this experiment took place has given its name to the term psychologists and sociologists use to describe such experimenter influence: the Hawthorne effect.)

Multiple Causation

Newspaper headlines such as these are not uncommon:

STUDENT KILLS SELF AFTER EXPULSION FROM COLLEGE

HONOR STUDENT GOES ON RAMPAGE

Friends stated that John Bright had been depressed over the death of his girl friend.

Implicit in both these statements is an assertion of simple cause and effect: The student killed himself *because* he was expelled from college; John Bright rampaged *because* his girl friend had died.

But if expulsion from college really causes suicide, in a straightforward cause → effect manner, then every student who is expelled from college must commit suicide, which is absurd. The actions of both students were obviously the result of *multiple* causes.

Similarly, many scared, bewildered people today are crying for "get tough" police action to stamp out crime, for an end of welfare to encourage self-sufficiency, and for "old-fashioned" discipline to teach kids respect for their elders. In each case, they have fastened tenaciously on *one* action as the *one* cause of a complex phenomenon with multiple causes.

The ability to recognize faulty causation is especially important because cause–effect reasoning plays such a crucial role in the conduct of our lives. Consider this report, published in a national "childbirth education" magazine:

> A recent study of two hundred home deliveries in Isabella County, Michigan, reported only 2 percent of the mothers had complications during childbirth. For the same period, the hospitals in the area reported that almost 10 percent of the mothers experienced complications during childbirth.

The statistics cited were extensively documented: Factually, the report is true. But do these statistics support the conclusion that home birth is safer than hospital birth or the conclusion that hospital procedures increase the likelihood of a mother's having complications in childbirth? In short, do these statistics demonstrate a cause → effect relationship between hospital delivery and childbirth complications?

I hope that you answered both questions "No." In order for an affirmative answer to be warranted, the researcher would have to demonstrate that there were absolutely no differences between the two "populations" (home-birthing mothers vs. hospital-birthing mothers) except the *single* variable of where they delivered their children. No meaningful differences in average age, in prenatal care, in childbirth preparation, in prior birthing complications, and so forth.

As it stands, when used as "proof" of a cause → effect relationship, the report displays all three of the causation fallacies we've examined:

> *Oversimplification:* Many of the "predictors" of complications during childbirth are recognizable long before a woman goes into labor. It seems likely that obstetricians would urge women with potential birthing complications

to choose a hospital delivery instead of a home delivery. Thus, as in the Arizona respiratory deaths example, there are possible alternative explanations for the higher complication rate in hospitals.

Post hoc ergo propter hoc: The fact that a higher proportion of hospitalized women had birthing complications than did home-birthing women does not in itself establish a *causal* connection between such complications and place of delivery. After all, many times more Americans die in hospitals than die at home. But this correlation does not prove that hospitals cause death, whereas staying at home prevents death.

Hasty conclusion: Because the study cited does not include the additional information, statistics, and controls that we've discussed, it presents *insufficient evidence* to support a cause → effect conclusion.

NOTE: When you have shown that a conclusion or generalization does not logically follow from the evidence given, you have not automatically proven the conclusion to be false. In the example above, the question of whether or not home delivery produces lower complication rates than hospital delivery remains open—and unanswered. Both better research and better reasoning are needed to support a definitive conclusion one way or the other.

APPLICATIONS: FAULTY CAUSATION

1. The newspaper feature reprinted below summarizes a scientific debate concerning the possible cause–effect relationship between family size and the IQ of children. The research cited conclusively demonstrates that children from smaller families (two or three siblings) do indeed have higher IQs and complete more years of school, on the average, than children from larger families.

   As you read the article, record each *alternative explanation* cited and each acknowledgement of possible *multiple causation.*

   Do the researchers' findings strongly support the conclusion that small families *cause* higher IQ in children? Explain the basis for your answer.

   LOS ANGELES—Children in small families have higher intelligence quotients and complete more years of schooling than children from large families, even when family income is taken into account, scientists said Monday.

   One researcher noted that the nationwide upturn in Scholastic

Aptitude Test scores, which began in 1980, corresponds closely to the decrease in family size during the 1960s and 1970s, when children now taking the SAT were born.

The researcher, Robert Zajonc of the University of Michigan, predicted that SAT scores would continue to rise until 2000, when the children of today's larger families will show another decline.

He was one of a panel of researchers who discussed their studies at the annual meeting of the American Association for the Advancement of Science.

Zajonc said his research shows that the larger the number of children in a family and the shorter the spacing between them, the less their intellectual maturity.

He cautioned, however, that it would be unwise to base decisions on family size on his research.

"I would not advocate any pattern of spacing or children because many other factors are completely unknown," he said.

The unknowns include the effect of family size on a child's sociability, morality and ability to cope, he said.

Judith Blake of the University of California in Los Angeles used data on 54,000 children to show that the smaller the family, the more years of schooling the children will receive.

"The advantages of coming from a small family are gigantic—by that I mean two or three children," she said.

Her research shows a difference between families of two or three children and families of six or eight children, she said, but it does not as clearly show whether having two children might be better than having three.

Blake said her data showed that differences in income between large and small families were not important.

Furthermore, she said, the negative effect on children in large families occurs in grade school, not in high school and college when family resources might be more strained.

James Higgins, of Michigan State University, disagreed somewhat with these findings. He argued that the parents of large families tend to have low IQs, so the children's IQs are merely a reflection of their parents' and are not related to family size.

The researchers also disagreed whether a child with no siblings has an intellectual advantage over a child with brothers or sisters. Blake found that an only child had an advantage over children in a two-child family. Zajonc found the opposite.

The reason, he said, is that the only child has no younger sibling to come to him for help, something that can boost a child's maturity.

"This child is deprived of the chance to serve as an intellectual resource," Zajonc said.

He also said that the apparent dependence of years of education and IQ on family size does not mean that quality of schooling is unimportant.

"The rise and fall (of SAT scores) may follow the curve of family size, but how much they rise and fall depends on how much better we educate our youth," he said.

"There are many factors which affect the SAT. This is one that can be measured."

By Paul Raeburn, Associated Press,
Detroit Free Press.
May 28, 1985, p. 4A. Used by
permission of The Associated Press.

2. Explain the nature of the causation fallacy or fallacies in the following arguments. As you study each argument, ask yourself:

Is there possibly an *alternative explanation(s)* for the cause → effect relationship alleged?

Is the effect or phenomenon that is ascribed to a single cause possibly the result of *multiple causes?*

Could the alleged cause → effect relationship be merely a *correlation* instead?

Is a *post hoc* fallacy ("after this, therefore because of this") involved?

Does the argument involve a *hasty conclusion* because the conclusion is based on inadequate evidence?

a. The vocabularies of one hundred male college students were scientifically measured. Five years after graduation, all of those scoring in the upper 10 percent had executive positions; none of those scoring in the bottom 25 percent had executive positions. If you want to be an executive, increase your vocabulary.

b. In a recent television season, the number of programs depicting violence rose sharply. In the same time period, the national crime rate also registered a sharp climb. If crime in this country is to be controlled, the amount of violence in television programs will have to be drastically reduced.

c. It is a simple fact that inner-city blacks commit proportionally more violent crimes than suburban whites. It's time we faced the unpleasant truth: Blacks are more prone to violence and crime than whites.

d. In many school districts where forced busing has been implemented, white children have fled to private or suburban schools. It is therefore quite obvious that busing causes less, not more, racial integration in the schools.

e. Medical studies have shown that alcoholics tend to be undernourished. Hence it would appear that a poor diet is a major contributor to alcoholism.

f. A study of 3,400 New Yorkers who had heart attacks showed that 70 percent of them were ten to fifty pounds overweight. Clearly, obesity causes heart disease.

g. If you want to have well-mannered, polite children, you should speak to them softly but firmly. That's how I treated my children, and they are very quiet and well behaved.

h. Dave used to be a lot of fun, but ever since he got married, he's changed. His wife must have really laid down the law.

i. "There is a distinct relationship between gun control and crime. The state with the most stringent gun control is New York, and the robbery and burglary rate there is 18 times as high as here [in Wyoming]. You wouldn't really want to think about burglarizing a home in rural Wyoming or Colorado, because there might be somebody around with a gun. . . ."

Resident of Pinedale, Wyoming,
May 1985

j. "I've always reckoned that looking at the new moon over your left shoulder is one of the carelessest and foolishest things a body can do. Old Hank Bunker done it once, and bragged about it: and in less than two years he got drunk and fell off of the shot-tower and spread himself out so that he was just kind of a layer, as you may say; and they slid him edgeways between two barn doors for a coffin, and buried him so, so they say, but I didn't see it. Pap told me. But anyway it all come of looking at the moon that way, like a fool."

Mark Twain, Huckleberry Finn

OVERGENERALIZATION

Closely akin to hasty conclusion, the fallacy of *overgeneralization* is a judgment about an entire class of people or things based on observation of only one or a few. Think of an ant supporting an elephant, and you get to the heart of overgeneralization. An ant-sized bit of observation or experience can't support an elephant-sized generalization.

Overgeneralization most frequently occurs when one moves from a *tentative* or *qualified* assertion toward an *unqualified* or *categorical* assertion. There's a world of difference between an appropriately qualified generalization, such as *"Some* students go to college just to have a good time," and more inclusive generalizations asserting that *most* or *all* students go to college for this reason. (A point to remember: If you say, "Today, students go to college to have a good time," your phrasing means *"all* students." If you actually mean "some" or "many" or "most," you must make the qualification explicit.)

Overgeneralization promotes stereotypic thinking, producing a simplistic, distorted world view in which all Communists are atheists, all football players dumb jocks, all French people sensualists, all used-car salespeople crooks, all children of broken homes disturbed delinquents, and so forth.

Yet the appeal of this sort of reasoning remains strong, its practice widespread. And understandably so, for generalization is a means of ordering experience, interpreting it, and managing it. Still we must be cautious.

At the root of overgeneralization is an unwarranted *inductive leap* from a qualified "may" or "could" to a sweeping "is" or "does"; a leap from a demonstrable "few" or "some" to an overstated "most" or "all." A leap, in short, from fact to falsehood.

Such unwarranted inductive leaps are typically grounded in an *insufficient* or *unrepresentative sample.* For instance, many people accept the generalization that "The children of famous people are usually mixed up." In support of this conclusion, they might offer as "proof" such examples as these:

Edward G. Robinson, Jr., has been repeatedly arrested for drunk driving.

John Barrymore, Jr., was charged with drunk driving and hit and run, and his half-sister, Diana, was an admitted alcoholic.

Charles Chaplin, Jr., has a police record for drunkenness.

Cheryl Crane, daughter of Lana Turner, killed her mother's lover.

Winston Churchill's daughter, Sarah, has been arrested for drunkenness and on drug charges.

The son of Mary Tyler Moore committed suicide.

A list of such "mixed-up" children of celebrities could probably be extended to fill a dozen or more pages. But what would such a list, however long, really prove? It would simply prove that *some* celebrities have mixed-up kids, as do some quite uncelebrated doctors, accountants, laborers, and professors. Only a *representative* sampling of the children of celebrities, carefully correlated with an equally representative sampling of the offspring of unfamous people and then subjected to rigid statistical analysis, would be capable of supporting with reasonable credibility the generalization "Celebrities *usually* have mixed-up kids."

APPLICATIONS: OVERGENERALIZATION

Each of the following arguments involves a factual statement and a conclusion based on the facts cited. For each argument, explain why the conclusion represents the fallacy of *overgeneralization*.

1. I know plenty of kids from broken homes, and all of them are mixed up. If you want your kids to grow up healthy, don't get that divorce!

2. "Dear Ann Landers: I always thought it was narrow-minded and mean of you to take such a strong stand against lonely-hearts advertisements. I changed my mind today when I read the Nashville *Banner*. It seems a man named Henry Joneson of Tomahawk, Alberta (Canada), answered an ad in an agricultural publication. The woman who was looking for a companion was Ada Wittenmyer, age 37. Henry, the 50-year-old owner of a 900-acre ranch, was lonesome and thought Ada sounded "interesting." He didn't realize his letters and checks were going to a prison until District Attorney General Kenneth Atkins called and told him that Ada had just been convicted of poisoning her fourth husband. She already was serving a 25-year term for poisoning her third husband—a wealthy Oklahoma rancher she had met through another lonely-hearts ad. Mr. Atkins said that when he told him the news Mr. Joneson said, 'Oh Lord.' "

October 18, 1984

3. When I was a child, a priest told the police about something one of my friends told him in the confessional. That taught me that priests can't be trusted.

4. Patients in mental hospitals should not be given jobs that make them necessary to the running of the institution. For example, a "patient–worker" was discovered to be a homosexual taking care of his harem!

5. "After my father's death years ago, my mother rented a house on the east side [of Detroit]. When we moved into the house, it was a mess. There were holes in the plaster, and it was very dirty. My mother plastered the holes and painted the entire inside. The land-lord never came to collect the rent; my mother always sent it in. After a year, the landlord came to see the house. When she saw how nice it looked, she promptly raised the rent. She told my mother that the house was worth more than she was paying. That was some way to treat a renter who took care of someone else's property. No wonder renters don't try to keep up the property they rent. After our experience, I don't blame them."

R. M., Atlanta, Letter to the Editor

6. Several of my friends have had the misfortune of seeing residences next to them converted into rooming houses for college students, and they have scarcely enjoyed a peaceful night's sleep since. If we value the quiet and integrity of our neighborhoods, we must oppose the granting of any more zoning variances permitting such use of formerly single-family dwellings.

7. So-called "personal leave" days are supposed to be used only for legitimate emergencies. But many employees regard personal leave days as so much additional paid vacation and make up the wildest stories to take advantage of them, costing their employers lots of money. In the face of such abuse, personal leave days should be abolished.

8. Despite all the talk about AIDS being noncontagious in normal social contact, there has been a documented case in which a mother contracted the disease from her AIDS-afflicted child. This proves that AIDS can be transmitted without the so-called "exchange of

bodily fluids." Therefore, AIDS-infected children should not be permitted to attend public schools.

9. Few people like the idea of polygraph examinations, but even fewer like the idea of our national security being jeopardized by spies within the military and government. In order to prevent future spy scandals, all civilian and military personnel with access to classified information should be required to take polygraph examinations on a regular basis.

10. As a mental health counselor, I've talked with scores of women who have had elective abortions, and many of these women have shared with me feelings of profound regret and sorrow about their decision. For the sake of the mental health and well being of women who become pregnant in the future, an anti-abortion amendment to the Constitution is needed.

FALSE ANALOGIES

False analogies are one of the most powerful weapons in the verbal arsenal of demagogues and are also responsible for some of the most brainless thinking around. "If you can't prove your point logically, use an analogy" is a rule all too many people follow, and all too many people are taken in by such use.

An *analogy*, when used in argumentation, is simply a *comparison* that argues that (1) *two* situations are similar in *certain* respects and (2) they are therefore similar in *other* respects also. Here are a couple of abbreviated analogies:

Leisure is like sugar. A little bit is sweet.

If a dog bites, club him! If a man commits a crime, imprison him!

If we were to trace out the argument implicit in the first analogy we would get something like this:

Leisure, like sugar, is pleasant only in small amounts. A lot of leisure is like too much sugar, unpleasant and cloying. So, be content with your two weeks' vacation a year and don't envy the beautiful people. These people just *seem* happy; really, they feel as terrible as you would if I forced you to eat five pounds of sugar!

Generally, when used illegitimately in argument, analogies are employed to *reinforce* attitudes the audience already holds. (The analogy just examined plays on the so-called Protestant ethic, which says that work is good and is the road to salvation, and on the quite understandable need of those people who *have* to work to feel that the "idle rich" really aren't happy anyway.)

A good rule of thumb is that analogies should never be used in argument as proof. If you use an analogy, use it only to *clarify* an assertion that has already been supported by relevant evidence and valid reasoning.

In "Yvonne and the Runaway Moms," if you recall, the analogy of looking at a mansion through various holes in a hedge was used to *clarify* the process of analysis, which involves looking at a subject from various points of view. In such a *clarifying* analogy, the reader is always aware of the essential differences between the two subjects being compared.

However, in the *argumentative* analogy, such crucial differences are glossed over, as in the following analogy that many people found quite convincing and "logical" during the early stages of the Vietnam War:

> If we had stood up to Hitler when he first began to move in Europe, World War II could have been avoided. Now the Communists are on the move in Southeast Asia. We cannot afford to make the same tragic mistake again.

When skillfully handled, the argumentative analogy can be quite seductive, *especially* if it reinforces a viewpoint or opinion we agree with. For example:

> Not everybody is allowed to drive a car. Not everybody is allowed to fly an airplane. Only those who have proved themselves competent, capable, and responsible are allowed to do so. Similarly, the sale and possession of firearms should be restricted to the competent, capable, and responsible.

A person who agrees with the conclusion to the above argument might well find the analogy perfectly "logical." Actually, however, the "competency" required for a driver's or pilot's license is a *skill-related* competency, whereas the "competency" to be required of gun owners has to do with *character* and *psychological* fitness—quite a different matter, and far more difficult to determine. This is precisely why argumentative analogies are fallacious: They ignore essential differences between the two subjects being compared.

Unfortunately, compelling others to recognize the illogic in an analogy—especially if it's one they've thought up themselves—is not always easy. There are two techniques, however, that will usually do the trick.

1. *Point out the negative analogy*—Pointing out the negative analogy means calling attention to the significant *differences* between the two subjects or situations that are being compared. That's what we did to show the illogic of the "driving is restricted—firearms should be restricted" analogy we just discussed.

2. *Extend the analogy to the point of absurdity*—This technique can be more fun than pointing out the negative analogy, because you impale the user of the analogy on his or her own sword, so to speak. We can demonstrate the procedure using this advertising slogan for a "high-protein" hair dressing:

> "Cut out grease. Put your hair on a low-calorie diet."

Extending the analogy—"Hey, that's a great idea. After all, a greasy diet can make a person fat, clog up the arteries with cholesterol, foul up the old metabolism. Let's see now, what are some low-calorie foods I can smear into my hair to keep it looking nice and healthy? Dry toast, that's the thing. How about a lettuce leaf or two . . . some bean sprouts . . . a cup of skim milk. Ahh. No more frizzies now."

CLARIFYING ANALOGIES

The benign cousin of the illogical argumentative analogy we've been discussing is the *clarifying analogy*. Unlike the argumentative analogy that tries to persuade you that two unlike things are the same, the clarifying analogy helps explain the unfamiliar by comparing it to something common and familiar. It says, in effect, "You will be better able to understand the unfamiliar subject I'm talking about if you think of it in terms of this familiar subject." In the following passage, the author uses a clarifying analogy to explain why the sky is blue:

> Imagine that we stand on any ordinary seaside pier, and watch the waves rolling in and striking against the iron columns of the pier. Large waves pay

very little attention to the columns—they divide right and left and re-unite after passing each column, much as a regiment of soldiers would if a tree stood in their road; it is almost as though the columns had not been there. But the short waves and ripples find the columns of the pier a much more formidable obstacle. When the short waves impinge on the columns, they are reflected back and spread as new ripples in all directions. To use the technical term, they are "scattered." The obstacle provided by the iron columns hardly affects the long waves at all, but scatters the short ripples.

We have been watching a sort of working model of the way in which sunlight struggles through the earth's atmosphere. Between us on earth and outer space the atmosphere interposes innumerable obstacles in the form of molecules of air, tiny droplets of water, and small particles of dust. These are represented by the columns of the pier.

The waves of the sea represent the sunlight. We know that sunlight is a blend of lights of many colours—as we can prove for ourselves by passing it through a prism, or even through a jug of water, or as Nature demonstrates to us when she passes it through the raindrops of a summer shower and produces a rainbow. We also know that light consists of waves, and that the different colours of light are produced by waves of different lengths, red light by long waves and blue light by short waves. The mixture of waves which constitute sunlight has to struggle through the obstacles it meets in the atmosphere, just as the mixture of waves at the seaside has to struggle past the columns of the pier. And these obstacles treat the light-waves much as the columns of the pier treat the sea-waves. The long waves which constitute red light are hardly affected, but the short waves which constitute blue light are scattered in all directions.

Thus, the different constituents of sunlight are treated in different ways as they struggle through the earth's atmosphere. A wave of blue light may be scattered by a dust particle, and turned out of its course. After a time a second dust particle again turns it out of its course, and so on, until finally it enters our eyes by a path as zigzag as that of a flash of lightning. Consequently the blue waves of the sunlight enter our eyes from all directions. And that is why the sky looks blue.[9]

See the difference? In this passage, the author is not trying to persuade us that air and water are the same, so how about a little skinny dip in the atmosphere. Instead, the comparison of sky to sea is used only to *clarify* the principles and concepts the author wants us to understand.

Use analogy only to clarify, and demand such restricted usage of other writers and speakers. If someone is arguing a point by analogy, *be suspicious!* The reason you should be suspicious is that very few situations or predicaments are exactly the same. And generally, the *differences* are more significant than the *similarities*. Analogy *ignores* the differences and hence ignores the complexity of the subject.

APPLICATIONS: FALSE ANALOGIES

1. For each of the following analogies:

    State the two subjects being compared.

    Indicate whether the analogy is argumentative or clarifying.

    Refute each argumentative analogy by (1) pointing out significant differences between the two subjects or (2) extending the analogy to show its absurdity.

    a. Comment by bar owner sued for serving drinks to an intoxicated customer: "I don't think a bar owner should insure drinkers any more than a grocery store should insure fat people."

    b. Dolby stereo is like a sonic laundry. It washes the dirt (or noise) out of the clothes (signal) without disturbing the clothes (signal).

    c. "Doctors come out with balanced diets, portfolio managers come out with balanced investments, deans go to work and come out with balanced curricula. Why can't scholars and writers come out with balanced reading lists?"

    William F. Buckley

    d. "The large-scale damage due to fire, drought, flood and other things has already presented the world with problems of reconstruction and reconstitution of biotic communities which are similar to those envisioned in the post [nuclear war] environment."

    Rand Corporation report

    e. "Back in the 1930s, the labor unions were like a 21-year-old woman. She was beautiful, had a gorgeous body, a sparkling personality, and she seduced a lot of people into the labor movement. That's fine. The problem is that this 21-year-old siren is now in her 60's and she's forty pounds overweight, needs a facelift, and has a terrible disposition."

    Eric Hoffer

f. "The number of people harmed because they don't wear seat belts is only a drop in the bucket compared to the thousands whose illnesses and deaths are attributed to smoking. As far as medical costs are concerned, there is no comparison.

"If it is going to be unlawful to risk one's life by not wearing a seat belt, then surely it should have to be unlawful to drink and smoke."

Letter to the Editor, Detroit Free Press

g. "Increasingly in the past few years, critics have warned that lawyers must be careful not to price themselves out of the market. We know what happens when that occurs in any field of activity: The consumers of the services or goods find other sources of supply. We saw that when the quality and price of the automobiles made in this country were found unacceptable. The consequences were very painful for our economy, and for our pride."

Warren E. Burger

h. If a boy is scared to stand up to a bully, his life will be hell. If we are scared to stand up to the Communists, we will have to live in a state of constant fear and dread.

i. This country has created an educational monster. Any business that produced such a shoddy product as that being produced by our schools would have long ago gone bankrupt for lack of customers. The schools cannot make exact specifications (other than age) for the "raw material" entering the educational system. What can be done is to sort the "raw material" periodically and discard that which is not up to the standard specifications.

j. Students should be in control of their education because it's their money. Students hire instructors to teach them; the instructors work for the students. How can it be, then, that the employee should put regulations on the employer? How can it be that the employee can penalize the employer? Thus, instructors have no right to require class attendance.

2. In the accompanying cartoon, what is the smug "moral" the affluent speaker is trying to argue by means of his analogy? Refute this analogy by pointing out significant differences between getting high or low grades on a report card and having a lot or a little money.

Explain how cultural conditioning plays a role in this analogy.

"Money is life's report card."
Drawing by William Hamilton; © 1979 The New Yorker Magazine, Inc.

SLIPPERY SLOPE

The fallacy of *slippery slope* is similar to the equally fallacious "domino theory" in foreign affairs. The slippery slope fallacy occurs when one argues that a certain action will lead to or justify a similar but less desirable action, which will in turn lead to or justify a still less desirable action, and so forth, down a "slippery slope" toward some horrible consequence. Because all reasonable persons must surely oppose the horror at the bottom of the slope, they should oppose taking the action, passing the law, or whatever, that will initiate (so the writer or speaker claims) the precipitous and disastrous slide.

It is fallacious to argue against an action on the unsupported assertion that it will lead to other, less desirable actions. A writer or speaker must convincingly demonstrate that one action will *necessarily* and *inevitably* lead to the horror at the bottom of the slope if that horror is to be accepted as relevant to an argument against taking the "first step."

Like all widely practiced and widely undetected logical fallacies, *slippery slope* has a certain superficial "common sense" appeal; to the uncritical mind, the slippery slope argument seems reasonable. Thus, it was widely argued (and widely accepted) that giving eighteen-year-olds the right to vote was unwise because, "Where would it stop? If eighteen-year-olds, why not sixteen- or fourteen- or ten-year-olds?" One critic pleaded for defeat of the proposal lest it lead to "carrying infants to the polling place to cast their pink or blue ballots."

When legislation to implement Medicare and Medicaid was before Congress, the American Medical Association lobbied against its passage on the grounds that the program would lead inevitably to the horror of "socialized medicine."

When the issue of allowing professionals such as doctors and lawyers to advertise their services and fees was being debated in the courts, opponents again resorted to the slippery slope argument. Such advertising would "demean and debase" these professions, leading to a "mad scramble" for clients. In the end, such crass materialism would deter caring and concerned individuals from entering these professions.

Of course, all three of these proposals have become law, and the "inevitable slide" has not occurred.

Today, the slippery slope argument is being used to oppose the passage of laws requiring registration of handguns, allowing voluntary euthanasia, and other social changes. Registering handguns, the National Rifle Association (NRA) contends, is but the first step toward banning private possession of weapons altogether. Then, the NRA concludes, once we have slid to the bottom of the slope, "When guns are outlawed, only outlaws will have guns."

APPLICATIONS: SLIPPERY SLOPE

Explain the nature of the slippery slope fallacy in each of the following examples.

1. Congressional approval of a national health care program would set a dangerous precedent. If socialized medicine, why not socialized airlines, socialized industry, socialized childcare? Soon, our heritage of free enterprise would be lost.
2. A Superior Court judge recently ordered a teenage boy taken away from his foster parents (two males) because it had been discovered

that the foster parents were homosexual. The foster parents, the boy, and a psychiatrist all testified that the relationship was warm and healthful, and that the foster parents had never made any sexual advances to the boy or attempted to influence his sexual orientation. In ordering the boy sent back to a state children's home, the judge explained that the boy could not be allowed to stay with the homosexual foster parents because, "If this were followed to a logical extreme, state action would be rationalized in placing promiscuous girls with prostitutes or psychopathic youths with the mentally ill and so on."

3. Prostitution should not be legalized because to do so would be to place the stamp of approval on criminal and immoral behavior. If we're going to legalize one type of crime, what's to prevent us from legalizing other types? Eventually, even murderers might be issued a state license giving them the right to kill.

4.

THE DRUNKARD'S DOOM

At dawn of day I saw a man
Stand by a grog saloon:
His eyes were sunk, his lips were parched,
O that's the drunkard's doom.

His little son stood by his side,
And to his father said,
"Father, mother lies sick at home
And sister cries for bread."

He rose and staggered to the bar
As oft he'd done before,
And to the landlord smiling said,
"Just fill me one glass more."

The cup was filled at his command,
He drank of the poisoned bowl,
He drank, while wife and children starved,
And ruined his own soul.

A year had passed, I went that way,
A hearse stood at the door;

I paused to ask, and one replied,
"The drunkard is no more."

I saw the hearse move slowly on,
No wife nor child was there;
They too had flown to heaven's bright home
And left a world of care.

Now, all young men, a warning take,
And shun the poisoned bowl;
'Twill lead you down to hell's dark gate,
And ruin your own soul.

Anonymous, from *Carl Sandburg,*
ed., The American Songbag

5. Allowing anyone without a Ph.D. degree to teach in college opens wide the gate to educational disaster. If the doctorate is not to be required of all professors, why then a master's degree, or a bachelor's degree, or even a high school diploma? When you pay hard-earned money to send your children to college, would you want them to be instructed by high school dropouts?

6. "If you don't control inflation . . . you will destroy the economy, and in a few weeks time there will be no food to buy, little water, no electricity and services, and there will be such panic and disaster that some hard-pants general is going to move in and say, 'I am now running the show,' and the Army or somebody like him will take over, and that's the end of the Constitutional Republic. And that's what's going to happen if we don't control inflation."

Texas State Senator Walter Mengden

7. "The dictionary defines 'crusade' as a remedial enterprise undertaken with zeal. People who act with zeal perforce are zealots, and zealots are first cousins of fanatics, and all of this is why the Rev. Donald Wildman [head of National Federation for Decency] and his followers give me the blue willies."

James J. Kilpatrick

8. "The proposal [to shift the cost of medicare to the general fund], if adopted, would begin the process of transforming Social Security

into an out-and-out welfare program. Once we start in that direction, where do we stop?"

New York Daily News

9. Lots of parents let their children have an occasional sip of wine or beer. Some even let their kids taste hard liquor such as gin or whiskey. But as the old saying goes, "One drink leads to another." If you want your children to grow up to be alcoholics, be "nice" to them and let them taste your drinks when company comes over.

10.

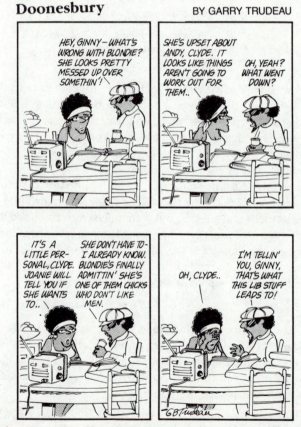

Doonesbury. Copyright 1976, G. B. Trudeau. Reprinted with permission of Universal Press Syndicate. All rights reserved.

2

Fallacies of Deduction

Deductive reasoning is argument that moves from general principles to specific applications, from premises to conclusion. But in order for the conclusion to follow logically from the premises, both premises *must* be absolutely, indisputably, categorically *true*. No matter if the premises are potentially true, or often true, or generally or usually or even nearly always true. That's not enough. One single exception to a *universal premise* (which is just a fancy term for blanket generalization) renders a deductive argument invalid.

Recall the argument cited on page 29:

Parents should think twice before getting a divorce because of the dire effects on the children.

Rewritten in the form of a syllogism, the argument looks like this:

(All) Divorce has dire effects on (all) children. (major premise)
(All) Parents should avoid dire effects on children. (minor premise)
(All) Parents should avoid divorce. (conclusion)

As you can see, the major premise of the argument is a blanket generalization. But because I know several children of divorced parents who seem happy and well adjusted, I can legitimately reject the major premise as unproven. Consequently, though the conclusion *may* be true, it does not follow logically and should not be accepted as a valid conclusion to this particular argument.

Most false deductive reasoning in real life follows this pattern. Specifically, such faulty reasoning involves:

1. a questionable generalization (major premise)
2. that is usually implied rather than stated
3. and is supported by culturally conditioned values or stereotypes.

To illustrate:

> Companies are justified in not hiring women for executive positions. If a woman executive became pregnant, it would cost the company a lot of money to find and train a new person to take over her job.

Here the questionable generalization (major premise) is "All working women who become pregnant quit their jobs and have to be replaced." The generalization does not appear in the argument itself; it is simply *assumed* to be true.

ENTHYMEMES

The fancy term for abbreviated deductive arguments, such as the two we have looked at so far, is *enthymeme*. Most frequently, it is the *major premise* that is omitted. One of the most useful skills you can develop is the ability to discover the hidden generalization in a deductive argument. For once you discover the suppressed premise and make it explicit, you can critically evaluate it.

Remember, such suppressed premises are *implied* rather than stated, yet they must be true *without exception* if the conclusion is to follow. If you can show the omitted major premise to be unproven, doubtful, or false, the conclusion does not logically follow. To illustrate:

> *Argument:* "Agricultural surplus is a permanent feature of the American scene."
>
> *Hidden Generalization:* "What has been true in the past is always true indefinitely into the future."
>
> *Discrediting:* Cite exceptions. For example, as of 1850, America had always had a frontier, but this did not mean a frontier was a permanent feature. As of 1965, America had never experienced an energy shortage, yet that did not mean it never would.

Remember that the exception does indeed prove the rule—it proves the rule *false*. If you can discover *one* exception to a categorical generalization, that generalization is false and must be rejected.

> *Argument:* "Women could serve in combat as well as men. After all, how many muscles does it take to launch an ICBM?"

Hidden Generalization: "All future wars will be nuclear and will involve only the firing of missiles by remote control."

Discrediting: The generalization is unproved and extremely dubious. To date, all wars the United States has fought have involved ground combat with conventional weapons. Because the argument is based on a doubtful assumption, the conclusion does not follow logically.

Argument: "The legalization of marijuana is supported by dropouts and anti-establishment types all over the country. As responsible tax-paying American citizens, we must strenuously oppose such ill-advised legislation."

Hidden Generalization: "Responsible, tax-paying Americans should not support policies advocated by dropouts and anti-establishment types."

Discrediting: Apply the generalization to other subjects. For example, "Americans should not support freedom of speech because such freedom is advocated by dropouts and anti-establishment types. (Of course, the argument above also contains other hidden generalizations—that dropouts and anti-establishment types are "bad," are irresponsible, don't pay taxes, and so on.)

NOTE: As you have do doubt perceived, once a hidden generalization (suppressed premise) is made explicit, various strategies can be used to discredit it. You can point out exceptions to it; you can show how it is merely hypothetical; you can "concretize" the generalization to show its absurdity.

On the other hand, you will sometimes encounter arguments that contain one or more implied generalizations that are not false. Fine. There's nothing wrong or reprehensible about hidden generalizations. What's important is the ability to recognize and test them.

Consider this argument: "Unless poisons are kept out of the air, more people will be killed just because they breathe." The statement contains three implied generalizations.

1. Poisons are presently in the air.
2. These poisons cause deaths.
3. People should not die just because they breathe.

The first two hidden generalizations are true; they are facts. The third hidden generalization is admittedly a judgment as well as a generalization, but one to which I, at least, cannot find a convincing exception. Hence I find the original argument logically sound, even though it contains several hidden generalizations.

Finally, we need to bear in mind that exposing a dubious or false generalization in an argument does not necessarily mean that the *conclusion* of the argument is not true or not, at least, defensible. For example, it *could be* that the use of marijuana should not be legalized; it *could be* that America will always have an agricultural surplus; it *could be* that women can serve as well in combat as men. But such conclusions *do not* follow from the arguments cited, because these arguments, as we have seen, are based on demonstrably false generalizations.

APPLICATIONS: ENTHYMEMES

For each of the following enthymemes:

Discover and state the suppressed premise or premises—the hidden generalization(s).

Explain why or how the hidden generalizations are dubious, unproven, or false.

a. "Prostitution is an established fact of today's society. Therefore, controls should be set up for its legalization."

student essay

b. "If automation continues to increase, a large part of our labor force will be left unemployed."

student essay

c. "Unless children are involved in sports, they will never learn to work as part of a team or find the true meaning of sportsmanship."

student essay

d. "Finding the true cause of alcoholism lies in the road ahead."

student essay

e. He was too young to die.

popular saying

f. "One study made by the [American Bar] association estimates that as many as 10 to 13 percent of the lawyers engage in some form of advertising. But some of this small segment treat this freedom as a release from all professional restraints and use it as a license. We see some lawyers using the same modes of advertising as other commodities, from mustard, cosmetics, and laxatives, to used cars."

Warren E. Burger

g. This meat can't possibly be spoiled. I bought it at the store just this morning.
h. John must be very bright. After all, he graduated from Harvard.
i. It's unfair to force business majors to waste their time taking required courses in the humanities. You don't meet sales quotas by quoting Shakespeare.
j. "Successful businessmen have large vocabularies. This book will teach *you* to increase your vocabulary."

advertisement

The truth of each of the following statements is considered self-evident by many Americans. Actually, however, each statement is a deductive argument based on an implied universal premise (a hidden generalization).

For each statement:

Identify the hidden generalization.

Explain how cultural conditioning supports the widespread acceptance of this generalization.

Postulate an exception to the generalization (thereby showing it to be unproven or false).

For example: "Why isn't a nice person like you married?"

Hidden Generalization: "All nice people are (or should be) married."

Cultural Conditioning: This is a couple society. Being married is preferable to being single. Everybody wants to get married. Etc.

Exceptions: Shawn is nice, but she likes living alone. John is nice, but after two divorces, he's determined to stay single. Etc.

a. Nothing ventured, nothing gained.
b. If at first you don't succeed, try, try again.
c. Don't marry until you find the right person.
d. If you want something done well, do it yourself.
e. It's always darkest just before the dawn.
f. Spare the rod and spoil the child.

g. Sticks and stones may break your bones, but words can never hurt you.

h. Absence makes the heart grow fonder.

i. A fool and his money are soon parted.

j. Dare to be great.

SWEEPING GENERALIZATION

The fallacy of *sweeping generalization* consists of stating a general *principle* and then applying it, inappropriately, to a specific case as though the principle were a *rule*.

For example: "Our Constitution says everyone should have the right to life, liberty, and the pursuit of happiness. Jails and prisons deprive people of their liberty. Therefore, all convicts should be released."

This fallacy gets its persuasive power from its *resemblance* to valid argument. But in valid argument, the rule, or major premise, is true always and without exception, as in the following classic syllogism:

All men are mortal.
Socrates is a man.
Therefore, Socrates is mortal.

In the fallacy of sweeping generalization, a principle that is often or usually true is treated as though it were universally true.

The National Rifle Association (NRA) has made effective use of this fallacy for many years, arguing that legislation to regulate or ban the sale of handguns would be a violation of our constitutional right to bear arms. Here, again, a general principle is treated as though it were an inflexible, universal rule.

All sweeping generalization fallacies involve a general principle and a specific case. The way to expose the fallacy is to show how and why the specific case is *an exception to the general principle.*

In the first example above, our "right" to life, liberty, and the pursuit of happiness applies only so long as we behave lawfully. In the NRA example, the "right" to bear arms does not extend to the right to bear *all types* of arms, without regulation or restriction. In the interest of public safety, private citizens are legally restricted from bearing such arms as bazookas and machine guns. The regulation of handguns may be desirable for similar reasons.

APPLICATIONS: SWEEPING GENERALIZATION

For each of the following arguments, explain how a general principle has been applied *inappropriately* to a specific case.

a. Statistically speaking, people who undergo major cosmetic surgery —such as having a large nose made petite or a weak chin made strong—have a higher divorce rate than the national average. If you're happy with your marriage, keep your spouse away from a plastic surgeon!

b. It has been shown that birth defects are strongly influenced by heredity. If you want a normal child, don't marry a person in whose family there have been any birth-defective children!

c. Obese men and women who manage to "slim down" often drastically change their life styles. So, if you're fat and miserable, start that diet!

d. Today's women are demanding equal rights, equal job opportunities, and equal pay. If they want all these things, then they should pay their share of the bill when a guy takes them out on a date.

e. Statistical studies have shown that college students who have cars get lower grades than those who don't. If you want your son or daughter to do well in college, sell that car!

f. "If seat belts are so effective, why do people have to be ordered to wear them? The people I know are smart enough to decide for themselves what they must do to be safe."

Letter to the editor, Detroit Free Press

g. Our country was founded on the principles of free enterprise and self-sufficiency. Doing for yourself instead of expecting others to do for you is the essence of capitalism. Therefore, welfare programs should be abolished.

h. I can't understand why the police arrested the Michigan man who shot up a snowmobile belonging to a trespasser on his property. After all, the land was posted and the snowmobiler had no right to be there.

i. In a democracy citizens are supposed to have free choice in the conduct of their lives, so long as they do not infringe on the rights of others. It's obvious, therefore, that the government has no right to pass laws requiring motorcyclists to wear helmets or motorists to wear seat belts, since such laws violate our right to free choice.

j. I realize there is a lot of debate about the legitimacy of high speed chases to apprehend speeding or reckless drivers. But the police are supposed to pursue and arrest lawbreakers. That's their duty. Therefore, high speed chases are clearly warranted.

EQUIVOCATION

The fallacy of *equivocation* occurs when the same term is used in two different senses in an argument. Though comically obvious in its more blatant forms, equivocation can also be quite subtle and deceiving. For example:

> In rejecting the principal's curricular suggestions, the School Board pointed out that Mr. ——— obviously lacked authority in educational matters. The recent misconduct in the lunchroom and disruptive activities in the halls were cited as evidence of this lack of authority.

In this argument the term "authority" is used in two different senses: (1) sound knowledge of educational theory and practice and (2) discipline and control of student behavior.

© 1985 United Feature Syndicate, Inc.

"Bonjour. Comment vous appelez-vous? Comprenez-vous? Shucks, boys, this poodle is no more French than I am."

As you can see, the fallacy of equivocation involves shifting the meaning of a key term without acknowledging that shift, and then reverting to the original sense of the term in the conclusion. Here's an even more subtle example:

> One of the major mandates of the press in a free society is to publish news that is in the public interest. There is no doubt about the public interest taken in the brutal murder of former Beatle John Lennon and the intimate details of his and Yoko Ono's bizarre relationship. Therefore, the press had a duty to publish these matters in the public interest.

In this argument, the term "public interest" is first used in the sense of "public welfare." In the second instance, however, the meaning shifts to "what the public is interested in or curious about"—a different meaning altogether. Far from being mandated to publish whatever the public is "interested in or curious about," the press is restricted by law from invading the privacy of citizens for no reason other than the titillation of its readership.

When equivocation occurs in an enthymeme, the shifted term may be entirely hidden, as in this example, which we first saw on page 103.

> Women could serve in combat as well as men. After all, how many muscles does it take to launch an ICBM?

Here, the shifted term is "combat." In the conclusion (first sentence), it is used in the sense of "infantry combat," but in the supporting rhetorical question, the meaning of the term "combat" has been narrowed to the act of pushing missile launch buttons in a nuclear war.

APPLICATIONS: EQUIVOCATION

For each of the following arguments:

Identify the "shifted" word or phrase.

Explain how the meaning of the shifted term changes in the course of the argument.

1. I don't see how any fair-minded person can take the position that hunting is cruel. After all, in Africa, lions and tigers hunt and kill thousands of helpless impala and zebras and monkeys every year, and nobody gets upset about their hunting.

2. Education involves both knowledge and the application of that knowledge: theory and practice. That's why I'm against sex education in grade school and junior high. How would you like your eleven-year-old daughter practicing what *she* learned in such a course?

3. The Food and Drug Administration was established to protect us against impurities and filth in our food. It's high time for us to have similar protection against filth in the movies we watch.

4. The crucial importance of staying ahead of the competition is a proven business principle. The kickbacks that our buyer paid helped us stay ahead of the competition, so I don't see how he can be blamed. He was operating according to a well-established business principle.

5. Certainly a respect for the life of others is crucial to the stability of any society. The pro-abortion movement does not respect the life of the unborn child and thus threatens the very foundation of our society.

6. "Every society is, of course, repressive to some extent. As Sigmund Freud pointed out, repression is the price we pay for civilization."

columnist John P. Roche

7. I don't understand why you oppose my dating John. He lives next door and, after all, the Bible says, "Love your neighbor."

8. If we're not free to drive at whatever speed we want to, then we're not the free people Americans once were.

9. The tiny fraction of solar energy which strikes the earth is sufficient to warm the entire planet. Obviously, if solar energy can heat the whole earth, it can heat your home.

10. I can't believe you think a horse worth $50,000 is bound to be better than one worth $500. After all, is a person worth a million dollars necessarily better than someone only worth a hundred thousand?

3

Fallacies of Relevance

Consumer advocate Ralph Nader first made his mark with a book about a General Motors car, the Corvair, titled *Unsafe at Any Speed.* The fallacies described in this chapter might be similarly characterized as "irrational in all respects."

Fallacies of relevance are foul-play. Like grabbing a face mask in a football game, they violate the spirit of fairness and do violence to the process of rational inquiry.

These fallacies might be more aptly named fallacies of *irrelevance,* because all of them involve bringing in some sort of irrelevant issue, often one that is emotionally charged. When we speak of an argument "degenerating into name calling" or "becoming bitter and acrimonious" or—as sometimes happens even in legislative assemblies—"erupting into violence," we can be virtually certain that fallacies of relevance helped fuel the conflagration.

AD HOMINEM

Literally argument "to the man," the *ad hominem* fallacy substitutes a personal attack for substantive discussion. It attempts to discredit another's argument or opinions by attacking that person's *character;* the implication is that the person is too contemptible to have worthwhile ideas.

In many cases, of course, a person's character *is* relevant to his or her competency to fill a certain job or political position. Ted Kennedy's behavior following the accident at Chappaquiddick raised doubts about the senator's honesty and about his ability to act wisely and rationally in a crisis, both of which are relevant to a person's fitness for the presidency.

But even if it were proven that Kennedy lied about the events of that evening, such a fact about his character would not be relevant to the value, accuracy, and merit of his *opinions* about domestic and foreign issues. Ideas, values, and views are independent of the character of the person espousing them.

Mockery, sarcasm, slander, innuendo, and name calling are all symptoms of the *ad hominem* fallacy. By making an opponent appear ridiculous or despicable, the speaker or writer attempts to achieve a "transference" to the opponent's ideas, viewpoint, or argument. But the strategy can backfire, as well it should. A famous case in point occurred during a debate between anti-evolutionist Bishop Samuel Wilberforce and pro-evolutionist Thomas H. Huxley before a meeting of the British Association for the Advancement of Science in the year 1860.

WILBERFORCE (*with barbed sarcasm*): And you, sir, are you related to the ape on your grandfather's or your grandmother's side?
HUXLEY (*somberly*): A man has no reason to be ashamed of having an ape for a grandfather or a grandmother. If I had the choice of an ancestor, whether it should be an ape, or one who having scholastic education . . . should treat not with argument but with ridicule the facts and reasoning adduced in support of a grave and serious philosophical question, I would not hesitate for a moment to prefer the ape.

Another term used to describe the *ad hominem* fallacy is "poisoning the well." Just as any water drawn from a poisoned well is poisonous, so any idea advocated by a contemptible person must be contemptible. But, unlike water, the quality and merit of ideas are independent of their source.

APPLICATIONS: AD HOMINEM

Identify and explain the *ad hominem* element in each of the following arguments.

1. If that's the way you think, you must have lettuce for brains.
2. The Equal Rights Amendment is just one more unworkable inanity dreamed up by female chauvinist piglets.
3. I can't believe you're actually taking Mary's advice about marriage seriously. Don't you realize she's been divorced twice?
4. Most psychology majors are neurotics who go into the field hoping to find themselves.

5. "The little dictator [Nicaraguan President Daniel Ortega] who went to Moscow in his green fatigues to receive a bear hug did not forsake the doctrine of Lenin when he returned to the West and appeared in a two-piece suit."

President Ronald Reagan, June 5, 1985

6. Have you ever known a feminist model or beauty queen?

7. To the Editor:
   "I am an alumna of CMU. Here in Philadelphia, I have heard of the drunken debacle that has been occurring yearly at the school. I am sure that every resident of Mt. Pleasant is angry and frustrated that a minority of snot-nosed brats (everyone of whom is financed by daddy, I'll bet) can pollute the community as they do.
   "These spoiled brats who, in all their collegiate wisdom, believe that drinking and destruction are synonymous with adulthood should, every one of them, be expelled from school. That they are supported in their Neanderthal behavior by some professors who are no more than elderly adolescents themselves is just one more disgrace for the school.
   "Why is the administration of CMU afraid of dealing harshly with the criminal activities of the little cowards? What, possibly, do they add to the school?"

The Morning Sun, May 24, 1985

8. "Why do so many political protestors tend to be, to put it mildly, physically ugly? . . . they are either too fat or too thin, they tend to be strangely proportioned. . . . Perhaps they are really protesting what they see when they look in the mirror."

Jeffrey Hart

9. Of course the millage increase is supported by all the teachers in the district, but that's to be expected. After all, it's their own nest they're trying to feather at the taxpayer's expense.

10. "The idea put about in the United States and elsewhere by people emotionally committed to a united Ireland that Britain is in Northern Ireland against the wishes of the people there is demonstrably false. Anyone advancing such views is either totally ignorant of the facts or deliberately irresponsible and mischievious."

Humphrey Atkins

APPEAL TO AUTHORITY

The fallacy of appeal to authority is really the flip side of *ad hominem*. In *ad hominem*, the position a person advocates is discredited (fallaciously) by an attack on his or her character. In *appeal to authority*, the views of a high-status individual are presumed true (fallaciously) simply because of that person's high repute.

The fact that someone has achieved high status, position, popularity, or fame does not guarantee that the individual's beliefs are true or wise. All logical arguments must be grounded in evidence and reasoning, not in social status. High office does not convey omniscience.

Basically, as the cartoon illustrates, the fallacy of appeal to authority represents an attempt to intimidate us into accepting a certain opinion solely because it is the opinion held by those who occupy a position of authority, rank, respect, or high office. It operates the principle according to: "What right does a nobody like you have to challenge the view of a somebody like him?" But, as history has demonstrated again and again, high office does not necessarily confer insight. Even wise men can be wrong.

"Aren't you being a little arrogant, son? Here's Lieutenant Colonel Farrington, Major Stark, Captain Truelove, Lieutenant Castle, and myself, all older and more experienced than you, and we think the war is very moral."

Drawing by Handelsman; © 1968 The New Yorker Magazine, Inc.

Citing Expert Opinion versus Appeal to Authority

Citing expert opinion to strengthen or support an argument is always legitimate and often necessary when we are writing or speaking about subjects outside our areas of personal expertise. To be credible, convincing and relevant, the expert opinion cited should meet several criteria:

1. *The expert's credentials should be known, accepted, and generally respected by his or her peers.* In other words, the person should be generally recognized as an expert. In this era of mail-order ministries and degrees, being known as the Reverend ———; ———, Ph.D.; or Dr. ——— doesn't necessarily imply expertise in anything except hypocrisy.
2. *The expert's testimony should relate to his or her area of authority.* The fact that Linus Pauling won a Nobel Prize in chemistry does not automatically make him an expert about other subjects, such as the medicinal qualities of vitamin C.
3. *The expert's opinion should reflect the* consensus *of opinion among other experts in the field.* When there is no consensus among experts about a matter, citing the views of only one group or position amounts to slanting and suppressing evidence.
4. *The expert should be free of strong personal interest in the position he or she is advocating.* That's why we trust Underwriters Laboratory and *Consumer Reports* ratings of products more than the manufacturer's claims. Even though the manufacturer of a product is obviously an authority about that product, its testimony is tainted by self-interest and hence susceptible to bias.

Endorsements

Advertisers recognize and utilize the effectiveness of celebrity "endorsements" in selling their products. Such ads are often cited as examples of fallacious appeal to authority, inasmuch as they typically violate all four of the criteria for legitimate expertise.

On the other hand, it's difficult to imagine that anyone of average or higher intelligence really believes that Johnny Carson is an expert on clothing or Sandy Duncan on nutrition or Phyllis Diller on dental adhesives. It is more likely that celebrity endorsements derive their power and effectiveness from a subliminal act of identification and incorporation on the part of the audience—like the Indian practice of counting coups or the cannibalistic ritual of eating the heart of a brave enemy, an act presumed to transfer the vanquished individual's admired virtues to the victor. By wearing Johnny Carson suits or munching

Wheat Thins or gluing our dentures with Polident, we magically acquire at least one thing in common with a person we admire and wish to be like. Voodoo and celebrity endorsements have a lot in common.

APPLICATIONS: APPEAL TO AUTHORITY

Evaluate the following arguments. Which ones strike you as legitimate citing of expert opinion? Why? Which ones do you find to be fallacious appeals to authority? Why? Among the fallacious arguments, indicate those that violate one or more criteria for legitimate expert opinion and those that seem primarily intended to intimidate the opposition.

1. "Does pre-nuptial pact lead to divorce? Barbara Walters, engaged to TV production firm executive Merv Adelson, ran into Marvin Mitchelson at a Manhattan disco over the weekend, and asked the palimony lawyer about the wisdom of pre-nuptial agreements. Advised Marv: 'I never heard of a couple making a pre-nuptial agreement in which they didn't eventually get a divorce. It takes the romance out of marriage, signing an agreement.' Walters is reportedly still weighing the issue."

   news feature

2. How can you reasonably object to the new curricular proposal? After all, it's supported by the president, the provost, and all the other top administrators.

3. Fluoridation causes gum disease. Many eminent authorities, such as Dr. H. K. Box, University of Toronto, and Dr. G. C. Geiger, Florida Dental Health officer, have observed a marked increase in periodontal (gum) disease where small amounts of fluoride occur naturally in water.

4. "The Mont Blanc Diplomat—Many pen experts here and abroad consider the Diplomat to be the finest pen ever designed. It's Europe's most prized pen, unmatched in writing ease."

   advertisement

5. *Shakespeare of London* by Marchette Chute: "The best biography of Shakespeare."

   Bernadine Kielty, Book-of-the-Month Club News

6. How can anyone question the sanctity of marriage? The institution of marriage is as old as human history.

7. "Felicia Munoz: 37. Profession: conductor. Hobbies: painting, attending concerts. Profile: vigorous; chic; exciting; conducts with a sure command of her music and her musicians. Scotch: Robbie Burns."

advertisement

8. "Hospitals use Tylenol more than other non-prescription pain relievers."

advertisement

9. I don't think you should buy an Omni. A friend of mine told me they have a bad repair record.

10.

"Let me tell you, folks—I've been around long enough to develop an instinct for these things, and my client is innocent or I'm very much mistaken."

Drawing by Handelsman; © 1985 The New Yorker Magazine, Inc.

AD IGNORANTIAM

Literally an appeal "to ignorance," *ad ignorantiam* is the fallacy of claiming something is true because it cannot be disproved or that something is untrue because it cannot be proved. For example:

Mental telepathy exists because you can't prove it doesn't exist.

The burden of proof for a generalization always rests on the person making the assertion. Argument *ad ignorantiam* says, on the other hand, "Because you can't prove I'm wrong, I'm right."

A variance of this fallacy argues, "Because you can't prove you're right, you're wrong." (If you can't prove it's true, it's false.)

If you happen to believe in astrology, in the value of casting stones, in the concepts of "aura" or karma, or in virtually any belief system out of the western "scientific" mainstream, you've probably encountered skeptics who have challenged you to "prove" the accuracy of your belief —and who concluded from your inability to do so that your belief was nonsense (that is, false).

Ironically, such individuals are also committing the fallacy of *ad ignorantiam*, because the burden of proof for their skepticism rests on *them*, not on you.

A couple of decades ago, when reports about the Chinese use of acupuncture in medical treatment first began to filter into the United States, the procedure was rejected and ridiculed by the American medical establishment. After all, whoever heard of anesthetizing patients by sticking them with needles? Besides, there were no scientific studies in reputable Western medical journals demonstrating acupuncture's effectiveness. Of course, the reason there were no such reports was that, at the time, no Western physicians had employed acupuncture.

So *ad ignorantiam* cuts both ways. You can't prove a positive with a negative ("God exists because you can't prove he doesn't"). But neither can you prove a negative with a negative ("There's no such thing as karma because you can't prove there is").

APPLICATIONS: AD IGNORANTIAM

Explain how each of the following arguments reflects the fallacy of argument *ad ignorantiam*.

1. If evolution is true, why has it stopped?
2. If you think psychokinesis isn't possible, then how do you account for Uri Geller's ability to bend keys just by looking at them?
3. Even though not required to do so by law, I have made full disclosure of my financial history to the public. My opponent's refusal to do the same is clear evidence the he has some shady dealings to hide.
4. "No medical evidence or scientific endorsement has proved any other cigarette superior to Sussex."

advertisement

5. If there were such a thing as the human soul, then certainly doctors, who have dissected every part of the human body, would have discovered it.

6. Of course, we hear talk about the evil machinations of an international criminal conspiracy dubbed the Costa Nostra. But what do you expect from law enforcement agencies seeking bigger budgets? The plain fact is that there's never been documented proof that the so-called Costa Nostra exists at all.

7. I know the stars influence the way people are. Can you prove they don't?

8. I'm amazed at your contention that Lee Harvey Oswald acted alone in killing President Kennedy. Why, even the special Presidential Commission that investigated the assasination was never able to prove there was no conspiracy.

9. Of course God exists. The existence of the universe proves it. If He didn't create it, who did?

10. Linus Pauling says vitamin C cures the common cold, and that's good enough for me. After all, Pauling's contention hasn't been proved wrong.

BANDWAGON

Which would you rather be, "one of the group" or "an outsider"? A "joiner" or a "loner"? We are social beings. It feels good to belong, to be included, to be part of the action. It feels uncomfortable to be excluded, left out, isolated, and alone. Hence the insidious appeal of the *bandwagon* fallacy: "Everybody's doing it; therefore, it must be good."

Television and magazine advertisements make wide use of the *bandwagon* appeal, saying in effect, "Look at all these nifty, happy people guzzling Bud or chugging Pepsi. Look at all these handsome, fast-track Yuppies puffing Player cigarettes. Don't be left out. Hop on the bandwagon."

Bandwagon is a sort of democratized variant of appeal to authority. Where the former exploits our respect for experts and leaders, bandwagon exploits our respect for the common sense of the common man. After all, twenty million Americans can't be wrong, can they? Yes.

APPLICATIONS: BANDWAGON

Explain the nature of the *bandwagon* fallacy in each of the following arguments.

1. "In Philadelphia, nearly everyone reads the *Bulletin.*"

    advertisement

2. "99 out of 100 new homeowners heat with gas."

    advertisement

3. "Now. A fantastic new novel by America's number one best-selling author."

    advertisement

4. "Sony. Ask anyone."

    advertisement

5. "Every nation has as one of its major sovereign rights the right to control the flow of people into its country. Of the 165 nations on this planet, 164 do so rigidly. Only the United States has a lax immigration policy."

    Charles R. Stoffel

6. "Gordon's Gin. Largest seller in England, America, the world."

    advertisement

7. "Darling, have you discovered Masterpiece? The most exciting men I know are smoking it."

Eva Gabor, in ad for Masterpiece pipe tobacco

8. "Eight out of ten headache sufferers use Bayer aspirin to relieve headache pain. Shouldn't you?"

advertisement

9. Don't miss out. See "Out of Africa"—the movie *everybody's* talking about.

10. Lots of other universities have recognized the need to evaluate college teaching and have established committees to do so. It's the coming thing.

COMMON PRACTICE

Common practice is the fallacy of justifying a course of action on the grounds that it is widely practiced by others. Almost always, the action rationalized by appeal to common practice is acknowledged to be wrong or reprehensible.

Although at first glance the fallacies of bandwagon and common practice may seem similar, they differ significantly. The essence of bandwagon is "What's popular is right." The essence of common practice is "Two wrongs make a right."

In the summer of 1985, when President Reagan announced that his administration would no longer comply with the provisions of the historic SALT II treaty, the fallacy of common practice was employed to justify the decision: the Russians were not complying with all the terms of the treaty (that is, violations were common practice). Therefore, America should not comply either.

In 1983 and 1984, when several U.S. corporations were indicted (and later convicted) for having bribed members of foreign governments in order to secure lucrative contracts, they defended themselves on the grounds that bribery was part of standard business procedure (common practice) in these countries. When the brokerage house of E. F. Hutton was charged with "kiting" hundreds of millions of dollars worth of checks in order to avoid paying interest on these funds, the company admitted it had done so but alleged that many other financial institutions did the same thing (common practice), though on a lesser scale.

Of all the fallacies discussed in this section, *common practice* is perhaps the most reprehensible. It is typically used as a self-serving rationalization for actions difficult, if not impossible, to justify rationally and reasonably. Of all the fallacies examined, *common practice* comes closest to being an *excuse* rather than a *reason*.

APPLICATIONS: COMMON PRACTICE

Explain how each of the following arguments attempts to justify and excuse a reprehensible course of action via the appeal to common practice.

1. There's nothing wrong with fudging a bit on your income taxes. Lots of people do it.
2. I don't see why you should be so upset. After all, it's not like I'm the first guy in the world to have an affair.
3. The company isn't going to go bankrupt just because I take home a little something. Inventory shrinkage is a fact of life in any business.
4. Where there's a booming business, there a booming market. These "research aid" services for students are springing up all over the country. Why should I flunk a course when other students in my situation are submitting research papers they bought and are getting *A*'s.
5. I don't understand your indignation about the President's impounding funds voted by the Congress. Every recent President has done the same thing.
6. I don't see what's wrong with using hidden notes in a test. After all, most students cheat in school, one way or another.
7. Just because I like to unwind with a few cocktails after a hard day's work doesn't mean I have a drinking problem. Lots of people I know drink more than I do.
8. Get off my back about speeding. Plenty of other drivers are going just as fast as I am.

9. Why should I have to get sick to enjoy a paid day off now and then? I know plenty of other guys at work who call in sick when they're really not.
10. Let's face it, a picket line just isn't enough to deter scabs. A few broken windshields are necessary to make them see the light. In any long strike you've got to expect a little violence. It's typical.

EMOTIVE LANGUAGE

The capacity of emotionally charged language to short-circuit reason and objectivity has long been recognized by demagogues. In fact, such language can be so "reason-preemptive" that some expressions are often called "fighting words."

In his book *Language in Thought and Action,* linguist S. I. Hayakawa gives us useful classifications for emotive language: *snarl* words and *purr* words. Snarl words are those with highly unfavorable connotations, such as "butchery," "slavery," and "rampage." Purr words, in contrast, have strong positive connotations, such as "justice," "responsibility," and "freedom."

Emotionally charged language can block clear thinking in a number of subtle and not-so-subtle ways. First of all, much emotive language is *figurative,* meaning that words are not used in their usual, literal, or exact sense:

He doesn't have any *guts.*

Americans should be proud of their *flag.*

The italicized words are examples of figurative language. Notice how such language is, literally speaking, false. For all people have intestines ("guts"), and the speaker in the second statement doesn't mean that we should unfold the American flag when company comes and proudly admire the stitching and the vividness of the colors.

At first glance, figurative language seems quite different from abstract language because it is *concrete,* it *appeals to the senses.* We can see "flag" and picture and touch "guts." But because figurative language is *literally false,* it doesn't mean what it says. Therefore, it is *vague* and *imprecise* and *ignores the complexity of the subject* just as an unconcretized abstraction is vague and imprecise and ignores the complexity of a subject.

Another way figurative language is similar to abstract language is that, although it *says* something concrete, it often *means* something abstract. Thus "He doesn't have any *guts*" (figurative language) *means* "He doesn't have any *courage*" (unconcretized abstraction); "Americans should be proud of their *flag*" (figurative language) *means* "Americans should be proud of *America*" (unconcretized abstraction).

Emotive language also tends to be *prejudicial.* By employing language highly charged with either positive or negative connotations, speakers and writers can "slant" an issue in the direction they want even as they "present" that issue. Late F.B.I. Director J. Edgar Hoover once observed that "America is threatened by the rapidly growing, menacing two-headed monster of subversion and lawlessness." The issue in this case is whether or not subversion and lawlessness are rapidly increasing. In the emotion-charged metaphor with which Hoover presented that issue, the answer is already assumed to be "yes," *and* the supposed increase is characterized as a menacing, grotesque "monster." Note also the insidious analogy. A "rapidly growing, menacing two-headed monster" possesses no constitutional rights and is, in fact, subhuman. Any and all means are justified in order to exterminate such a "fiend." The analogy similarly suggests that we should ruthlessly pursue and exterminate lawbreakers and "subversives."

When you encounter arguments couched in emotive language, you should exercise special wariness. Of course, impassioned writing and speaking are not necessarily illogical. A deeply committed person with strong feelings about an issue may use emotive language to give extra force and impact to a logically sound and well-reasoned argument. So long as emotionally charged language coexists with sound argument, fine.

But such writers and speakers are probably in the minority. All too often, when emotive language predominates, sound is substituting for sense, emotion is running roughshod over reason.

APPLICATIONS: EMOTIVE LANGUAGE

1. Turn back to "Yvonne and Rock Normal," pages 16–21. List at least three instances of emotive language from Rock Normal's paragraph

on marriage and at least five from Yvonne's parody of his paragraph. How do these figurative terms reinforce the view of marriage each is trying to present?

2. Find and underline the emotive language in the following statements. Explain how each figurative term is literally false and how it "slants" the issue unfairly.

a. Criminals should not be coddled.

b. The local storm troopers of our police department have pulled another of their neo-Nazi atrocities.

c. No man with any backbone wants a woman to fight his nation's battles.

d. A definition of prayer: "Someone is gibbering away on his knees, talking to someone who is not there."

R. D. Laing

e. "Just south of our border we face a major challenge to democracy and our security from Soviet-sponsored subversion and aggression. . . . The Soviet bloc nations and their terrorist allies are pouring in weapons and ammunition to establish a beachhead on our doorstep."

Ronald Reagan

f. "We dare not allow America to become weak and defenseless because if we do, the day could come when we would not be divided into hawks and doves—just pigeons."

Ronald Reagan

g. "While millions of miserable straights wither in the nine-to-five confinement of their deadly routines and responsibilities, bikers are out in the world packing more life into one day than most citizens will experience in a year."

Tex Campbell

h. "Immorality in all its corrupting aspects is sweeping through our country like a wild and uncontrollable hurricane."

letter to the editor

i. Who can excuse the brutal slaughter of innocent baby seals by greedy killers anxious to sell the pelts to furriers catering to the idle rich?

j. "You can have a vital part in our patriotic campaign on behalf of the Real America . . . the land of brave, proud, confident, hardworking people. Your tax-deductible contributions can multiply our efforts. You can help guide our youth along good pathways and fight the one-world socialists who would sell us out."

circular

RED HERRING

In argument, the fallacy of raising an irrelevant issue to divert attention from the primary issue is called the red herring fallacy. For example:

Argument: "Ex-convicts should have all their civil rights restored after serving their term of imprisonment."

Red herring rebuttal: "Would you want your daughter to marry a convicted killer?"

In popular usage, the term "red herring" means something that throws you off the track, and indeed, the name derives from the old hunting practice of dragging a herring across the trail of an animal in order to throw pursuing dogs off the track.

Other names for this fallacy—*ignoring the issue* and *diversion*—point to its essential quality, that of *ignoring* the issue at hand and *diverting* the argument onto a different issue. For example:

All of this talk about a nuclear freeze in order to save the world from a nuclear holocaust is absurd. After all, even if we froze the levels of nuclear armaments this very day, there would still be enough warheads to destroy civilization many times over.

Typically, the red herring fallacy gets its persuasive power from the fact that its conclusion, as in the foregoing argument, is true. But though such a conclusion may be true, it is irrelevant to the original issue. Nuclear freeze advocates see the freeze as a necessary first step in the scaling down of the arms race, a precondition for subsequent steps that could result in a reduction of the worldwide nuclear arsenal.

APPLICATIONS: RED HERRING

Explain the "red herring" element in each of the following arguments. In doing so, identify the "false trail" or irrelevant "new issue" the writer or speaker raises in order to *divert* the argument from its original focus.

1. I'm a hunter, and I'm sick and tired of hearing people claim hunting is a cruel sport. After all, if you were a deer, which would you prefer to be killed by—a gunshot or a lion?

2. I can't understand your objections to a 1:00 A.M. curfew in the women's dorms. We used to require women to be back in the dorms by 10:00 P.M. So you're lucky. You get to stay out a lot later than they did.

3. The candidate is an honest man. He likes sports, has a loving wife, and plays with his children on weekends.

4. Argument in support of capital punishment: "Where would Christianity be if Jesus got 8 to 15 years with time off for good behavior?"

    New York State Senator James Donovan

5. So you favor letting oil companies expand their offshore drilling along our beautiful coast. Don't you care at all about the quality of life for future generations?

6. The idea of registering handguns is preposterous. Was the American West won with registered guns?

7. How can you take that article seriously? After all, it was published in *Playboy*.

8. Women ought to be required to serve in combat. Why should men be the only ones to face danger and death?

9. Limits have got to be placed on "pain and suffering" awards by juries in personal injury and product liability lawsuits. How much pain and suffering do you think a lawyer experiences when he collects one third to one half of a million dollar settlement?

10. So, you're pro-abortion, are you? How would you feel if your mother had decided to abort *you?*

TU QUOQUE

Meaning "You, too" or "You're another," *tu quoque* is the defensive counterpart to *ad hominem*. For example, in an argument over a proposed increase in the school tax, one person might say, "The only reason you support it is that you've got four kids in school." This is a form of the *ad hominem* fallacy because the charge ignores the issue and suggests the proponent is selfish and self-serving. A *tu quoque* response might run: "The only reason you're against the increase is that your children have finished school." Hence, in effect, "If I have selfish motives, so do you."

The most common form of *tu quoque* involves an attempt to discredit an opponent's opinion or position by alleging that his *actions* contradict his *words:* that he doesn't practice what he preaches.

For example: "Who are you to advise me about the dangers of smoking? You puff your way through two packs a day."

Like most forms of fallacious reasoning, the *tu quoque* fallacy is easy to spot when we disagree with the position of the person committing the fallacy. Thus, in the example above, it is obvious that whether or not a person smokes is irrelevant to the point that smoking endangers one's health. But when we *agree* with the position of the writer or speaker committing the fallacy, its irrelevance is not always so readily apparent. For example:

> You're always criticizing the social welfare policies of our government and praising the way Denmark and Sweden provide "cradle to grave" security for their citizens. If you really believe those countries are so great, why don't you go live there?

Tu quoque is reminiscent of the challenge to "Put your money where your mouth is." But the fact is that whether or not a person *acts* on the basis of a principle or view or opinion is irrelevant to the merits of the idea itself.

APPLICATIONS: TU QUOQUE

Explain the nature of the *tu quoque* fallacy in each of the following arguments.

1. Don't give me a lecture about the dangers of drinking and driving. You treat yourself to a cocktail hour nearly every day and then drive wherever you please.

2. Okay, okay. I admit I occasionally do a bit of shoplifting. But you have no right to criticize me. Every time you file your tax return, you pad your business expense deductions.

3. It's not fair to punish me for hitting Sally. She hit me first.

4. Don't get on my case about turning in a research paper I didn't write. I remember how you lied about your parents' income on the student aid application.

5. Your argument against the practice of giving academic awards to honors students is hypocritical. After all, you didn't turn down your Phi Beta Kappa award when you were an undergraduate.

6. Speaker A: "Stop yelling at me. The only way to solve this problem is to talk calmly about it."
   Speaker B: "Well, you don't yell! You just cry all the time. Do you think that's any better?"

7. "It takes one to know one."

   popular saying

8. Of course, obtaining justice for poor people in this state is a problem. But it's just as much of a problem in your home state, as well.

9. "People who live in glass houses shouldn't throw stones."

   popular saying

10. Who are you to tell me how to run my life? You're not exactly perfect yourself, you know.

APPEALS TO PITY AND FEAR

As the names of these two fallacies suggest, both attempt to sway us by zeroing in on a single primal emotion. The *appeal to pity* exploits our noble side—our capacity for altruism, empathy, sympathy, and compassion. The *appeal to fear* exploits an even more elemental emotion—our survival instinct, our terror of injury, illness, assault, poverty, disaster, and death.

As illustrated in the cartoons, appeals to pity try to *guilt* us into a certain course of action, and appeals to fear attempt to *scare* us.

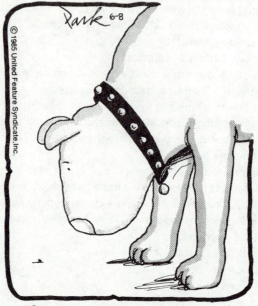

"Gee, you wouldn't turn away one lonely, pregnant flea, would you?"

You don't have to be a psychologist to recognize that inducing guilt and threatening people are *manipulative* and *coercive* strategies. Any young person who has been on the receiving end of a parental statement such as "How could you do such a thing to your mother?" (or father) understands the power of an appeal to pity. Any young person who has been told, "If you don't get off that phone this instant, you're grounded for a week," understands the power of an appeal to fear.

Note the essential feature of both examples. No reasons. No *rational, objective* discussion of the issue. Just guilt or threat. Just pity or fear.

APPLICATIONS: APPEALS TO PITY AND FEAR

Indicate which of the following arguments represent an appeal to pity and which represent an appeal to fear. In each instance, explain how the argument tries to make us feel guilty or scared.

1. You better be good
   You better not cry

BOY.

Drop out of school now and that's what they'll call you all your working life.

To get a good job, get a good education.

You better be nice,
I'm telling you why.
Santa Claus is coming to town.

2. "If you act quickly, you can have your copy of the one book that can really help you earn more, *before thousands of your competitors buy it in the bookstores!*"

circular

3. Doomed to suffer and die simply for human vanity. Baby harp seals are so beautiful that humans wish to wear their fur. Each year Canadian and Norwegian sealers come with their clubs. The pups cannot get away—less than one week old, they are too young to swim. Most never do. The pups are *clubbed and skinned before their mothers' eyes.* Only continued forceful public opposition can stop this insane killing. Write the Canadian and Norwegian ambassadors *today.*

circular

4. WITHOUT INSURANCE
YOUR LIFE
WOULD BE A DEATHTRAP

advertisement

5. "If you ever use that word in my presence again, I'll wash out your mouth with Lifebuoy soap."

my grandmother, when I was a boy

6. "American Express. Don't leave home without it."

7. "The feminization of the American male . . . Many men's fragrances make you smell like a bunch of lilies. Or fresh fruits. Or vanilla ice cream. Ascot makes a tough cologne, with the clean, fresh, masculine bite of spice. Ascot, because a man shouldn't smell like a woman."

8. "Aren't you glad you use Dial? Don't you wish everybody did?"

9. Michael, you really should ask my roommate, Cindy, to the dance next Friday. She hasn't had a date all year. Have you ever thought about what it would be like to sit alone in your room, while all your friends are out having fun?

10. Sure, you can try and unionize the shop, but don't blame me if you are permanently unemployed afterwards.

APPLICATIONS: LOGICAL FALLACIES

1. In the following dialogue, Yvonne's friend Nancy commits at least six of the logical fallacies we've examined in this section. After reading the dialogue:
   Identify by name each logical fallacy in Nancy's argument.
   Describe the technique that Yvonne uses to expose each fallacy.

YVONNE AND THE SPEED FREAK

Nancy, a former classmate of Yvonne's, recently purchased a new sapphire-blue Mazda RX-7 sports car and is making the rounds to show it off to her friends. When we join her, she has just knocked on the door of Yvonne's apartment.

YVONNE: Why, Nancy. What a surprise. Come in.
NANCY: Never mind that. Come out and see what I've got.

YVONNE (*following Nancy as she strides around the apartment building toward the parking lot*): It's really nice of you to stop by. I've called you a couple of times but you must have . . .

NANCY (*haltingsuddenlytogesturedramaticallyatthegleamingMazda*):TaTa!

YVONNE (*still recovering from the near miss of Nancy's swinging arm*): Uh. What?

NANCY (*boastfully*): Mine. All mine.

YVONNE (*beginning to understand the reason for Nancy's visit*): You've bought a new car.

NANCY (*gazing dreamily at the Mazda*): Isn't she beautiful?

YVONNE: Lovely.

NANCY (*impulsively*): Hey. I've got this great idea. Why don't you hop in and we'll see if we can set a record from here to Mortsburg. Really open her up. Come on. It'll be a blast.

YVONNE: I'd love to go for a ride with you. But only if you promise not to drive over 55. After all, that's the speed limit.

NANCY (*incredulously*): Not over 55? In *this* car? Why, that would be as ridiculous as hooking up an eighty-watt amplifier to the speaker in a five-buck radio.

YVONNE: I don't quite get the connection. Are you saying they're now making amplifiers equipped with engines and steering wheels and tires and . . .

NANCY (*smiling thinly*): Ha, ha. Funny. You always were sort of funny. Seriously, though, don't you realize that the whole 55-miles-per-hour business is nonsense? Why, as many people were killed on the highway last year as in 1973, the year before the speed limit was lowered. So much for the argument that driving 55 is safer than driving 70.

YVONNE: 1973 was a long time ago. A lot's changed since then. There are many more cars on the road. And cars are much smaller than they used to be. At any given speed, collisions in small cars are more serious than collisions in large cars. So with more cars on the road, and smaller ones at that, a reduced percentage of accidents could still produce a larger number of fatalities.

NANCY (*who has been drumming her fingers impatiently on the Mazda's sun-roof while waiting for Yvonne to run down*): Look at me. I always speed. So do plenty of my friends. And not one of us has had a bad pile-up. So don't talk to me about speeding being dangerous. If it was, we'd all be dead.

YVONNE (*mildly*): You're generalizing from the experience of a small number of people over a brief period of time. That's like arguing that cigarette smoking doesn't cause cancer because you have five friends who smoke and none of them have died of cancer. It's simply not logical.

NANCY (*huffily*): Not logical? You're the one who's not logical. If you think a 55-mile-per-hour speed limit is safer, then why aren't you for a limit of 45, or 35, or better yet, 25, or 15, or 5? If nobody drove faster than 5 miles per hour, we wouldn't have any highway fatalities at all. If you're for a maximum of 55 on the grounds of safety, then the only logical conclusion is that you should advocate a maximum of 5. Then we could all go back to riding horses.

YVONNE: I'm sorry, but it simply is not true that the arguments for reducing the highway speed limit from 70 to 55 also support reducing it all the way down to 5.

NANCY (*glowering*): Oh yeah. Well, let me tell you something. It's a tragic sign of these timid, cowardly times when a red-blooded American like me can be brutally robbed of her God-given freedoms by a gaggle of Nervous Nellies who would rather crawl across the countryside like slimy inchworms than soar across it like noble eagles!

YVONNE: Aren't you getting a bit carried away?

NANCY (*leaping into the Mazda and raging at Yvonne through the open window*): Carried away? You smart-alecky egghead. You chicken-livered inchworm. I can't believe I ever offered a ride to such an idiot in the first place. (*She peels out.*)

YVONNE (*to herself, as she turns back to her apartment*): I wonder what got her so upset?

2. In the humorous story that follows, two college students of an earlier era become enmeshed in a conflict of love and logic. As you read the tale, jot down the names of those fallacies that appear there but are *not* discussed in this section of the text. Then make up an argument illustrating each of these "new" fallacies.

LOVE IS A FALLACY*
MAX SHULMAN

Cool was I, and logical. Keen—calculating, perspicacious, acute and astute—I was all of these. My brain was as powerful as a dynamo, as precise as a chemist's scales, as penetrating as a scalpel. And—think of it!—I was only eighteen.

*"Love Is a Fallacy" by Max Shulman. Copyright 1951 renewed 1979 by Max Shulman and reprinted by permission of Harold Matson Co., Inc.

It is not often that one so young has such a giant intellect. Take, for example, Petey Bellows, my roommate at the university. Same age, same background, but dumb as an ox. A nice enough fellow, you understand, but nothing upstairs. Emotional type. Unstable. Impressionable. Worst of all, a faddist. Fads, I submit, are the very negation of reason. To be swept up in every new craze that comes along, to surrender yourself to idiocy just because everybody else is doing it—this, to me, is the acme of mindlessness. Not, however, to Petey.

One afternoon I found Petey lying on his bed with an expression of such distress on his face that I immediately diagnosed appendicitis. "Don't move," I said. "Don't take a laxative. I'll get a doctor."

"Raccoon," he mumbled thickly.

"Raccoon?" I said, pausing in my flight.

"I want a raccoon coat," he wailed.

I perceived that his trouble was not physical, but mental. "Why do you want a raccoon coat?"

"I should have known it," he cried, pounding his temples. "I should have known they'd come back when the Charleston came back. Like a fool I spent all my money for textbooks, and now I can't get a raccoon coat."

"Can you mean," I said incredulously, "that people are actually wearing raccoon coats again?"

"All the Big Men on Campus are wearing them. Where've you been?"

"In the library," I said, naming a place not frequented by Big Men on Campus.

He leaped from the bed and paced the room. "I've got to have a raccoon coat," he said passionately. "I've got to!"

"Petey, why? Look at it rationally. Raccoon coats are unsanitary. They shed. They smell bad. They weigh too much. They're unsightly. They—"

"You don't understand," he interrupted impatiently. "It's the thing to do. Don't you want to be in the swim?"

"No," I said truthfully.

"Well, I do," he declared. "I'd give anything for a raccoon coat. Anything!"

My brain, that precision instrument, slipped into high gear. "Anything?" I asked, looking at him narrowly.

"Anything," he affirmed in ringing tones.

I stroked my chin thoughtfully. It so happened that I knew where to get my hands on a raccoon coat. My father had had one in his undergraduate days; it lay now in a trunk in the attic back home. It also happened that Petey had something I wanted. He didn't *have* it exactly, but at least he had first right on it. I refer to his girl, Polly Espy.

I had long coveted Polly Espy. Let me emphasize that my desire for this young woman was not emotional in nature. She was, to be sure, a girl who excited the emotions, but I was not one to let my heart rule my head. I wanted Polly for a shrewdly calculated, entirely cerebral reason.

I was a freshman in law school. In a few years I would be out in practice. I was well aware of the importance of the right kind of wife in furthering a lawyer's career. The successful lawyers I had observed were, almost without exception, married to beautiful, gracious, intelligent women. With one omission, Polly fitted these specifications perfectly.

Beautiful she was. She was not yet of pin-up proportions, but I felt sure that time would supply the lack. She already had the makings.

Gracious she was. By gracious I mean full of graces. She had an erectness of carriage, an ease of bearing, a poise that clearly indicated the best of breeding. At table her manners were exquisite. I had seen her at the Kozy Kampus Korner eating the speciality of the house—a sandwich that contained scraps of pot roast, gravy, chopped nuts, and a dipper of sauerkraut—without even getting her fingers moist.

Intelligent she was not. In fact, she veered in the opposite direction. But I believed that under my guidance she would smarten up. At any rate, it was worth a try. It is, after all, easier to make a beautiful dumb girl smart than to make an ugly smart girl beautiful.

"Petey," I said, "are you in love with Polly Espy?"

"I think she's a keen kid," he replied, "but I don't know if you'd call it love. Why?"

"Do you," I asked, "have any kind of formal arrangement with her? I mean are you going steady or anything like that?"

"No. We see each other quite a bit, but we both have other dates. Why?"

"Is there," I asked, "any other man for whom she has a particular fondness?"

"Not that I know of. Why?"

I nodded with satisfaction. "In other words, if you were out of the picture, the field would be open. Is that right?"

"I guess so. What are you getting at?"

"Nothing, nothing," I said innocently, and took my suitcase out of the closet.

"Where you going?" asked Petey.

"Home for the weekend." I threw a few things into the bag.

"Listen," he said, clutching my arm eagerly, "while you're home, you couldn't get some money from your old man, could you, and lend it to me so I can buy a raccoon coat?"

"I may do better than that," I said with a mysterious wink and closed my bag and left.

"Look," I said to Petey when I got back Monday morning. I threw open the suitcase and revealed the huge, hairy, gamy object that my father had worn in his Stutz Bearcat in 1925.

"Holy Toledo!" said Petey reverently. He plunged his hands into the raccoon coat and then his face. "Holy Toledo!" he repeated fifteen or twenty times.

"Would you like it?" I asked.

"Oh yes!" he cried, clutching the greasy pelt to him. Then a canny look came into his eyes. "What do you want for it?"

"Your girl," I said, mincing no words.

"Polly?" he said in a horrified whisper. "You want Polly?"

"That's right."

He flung the coat from him. "Never," he said stoutly.

I shrugged. "Okay. If you don't want to be in the swim, I guess it's your business."

I sat down in a chair and pretended to read a book, but out of the corner of my eye I kept watching Petey. He was a torn man. First he looked at the coat with the expression of a waif at a bakery window. Then he turned away and set his jaw resolutely. Then he looked back at the coat, with even more longing in his face. Then he turned away, but with not so much resolution this time. Back and forth his head swiveled, desire waxing, resolution waning. Finally he didn't turn away at all; he just stood and stared with mad lust at the coat.

"It isn't as though I was in love with Polly," he said thickly. "Or going steady or anything like that."

"That's right," I murmured.

"What's Polly to me, or me to Polly?"

"Not a thing," said I.

"It's just been a casual kick—just a few laughs, that's all."

"Try on the coat," said I.

He complied. The coat bunched high over his ears and dropped all the way down to his shoe tops. He looked like a mound of dead raccoons. "Fits fine," he said happily.

I rose from my chair. "Is it a deal?" I asked, extending my hand. He swallowed. "It's a deal," he said and shook my hand.

I had my first date with Polly the following evening. This was in the nature of a survey; I wanted to find out just how much work I had to do to get her mind up to the standard I required. I took her first to dinner. "Gee, that was a delish dinner," she said as we left the restaurant. Then I took her to a movie. "Gee, that was a marvy movie," she said as we left the theater. And then I took her home. "Gee, I had a sensaysh time," she said as she bade me good night.

I went back to my room with a heavy heart. I had gravely underestimated the size of my task. This girl's lack of information was terrifying. Nor would it be enough merely to supply her with information. First she had to be taught to *think*. This loomed as a project of no small dimensions, and at first I was tempted to give her back to Petey. But then I got to thinking about her abundant physical charms and about the way she entered a room and the way she handled a knife and fork, and I decided to make an effort.

I went about it, as in all things, systematically. I gave her a course in logic. It happened that I, as a law student, was taking a course in logic myself, so I had all the facts at my fingertips. "Polly," I said to her when I picked her up on our next date, "tonight we are going over to the Knoll and talk."

"Oo, terrif," she replied. One thing I will say for this girl: you would go far to find another so agreeable.

We went to the Knoll, the campus trysting place, and we sat down under an old oak, and she looked at me expectantly. "What are we going to talk about?" she asked.

"Logic."

She thought this over for a minute and decided she liked it. "Magnif," she said.

"Logic," I said, clearing my throat, "is the science of thinking. Before we can think correctly, we must first learn to recognize the common fallacies of logic. These we will take up tonight."

"Wow-dow!" she cried, clapping her hands delightedly.

I winced, but went bravely on. "First let us examine the fallacy called Dicto Simpliciter."*

"By all means," she urged, batting her lashes eagerly.

"Dicto Simpliciter means an argument based on an unqualified generalization. For example: Exercise is good. Therefore everybody should exercise."

"I agree." said Polly earnestly. "I mean exercise is wonderful. I mean it builds the body and everything."

"Polly," I said gently, "the argument is a fallacy. *Exercise is good* is an unqualified generalization. For instance, if you have a heart disease, exercise is bad, not good. Many people are ordered by their doctors not to exercise. You must *qualify* the generalization. You must say exercise is *usually* good, or exercise is good *for most people*. Otherwise you have committed a Dicto Simpliciter. Do you see?"

"No," she confessed. "But this is marvy. Do more! Do more!"

"It will be better if you stop tugging at my sleeve," I told her, and when she desisted, I continued. "Next we take up a fallacy called Hasty Generalization. Listen carefully: You can't speak French. I can't speak French. Petey Bellows can't speak French. I must therefore conclude that nobody at the University of Minnesota can speak French."

"Really?" said Polly, amazed, *"Nobody?"*

I hid my exasperation. "Polly, it's a fallacy. The generalization is reached too hastily. There are too few instances to support such a conclusion."

"Know any more fallacies?" she asked breathlessly. "This is more fun than dancing even."

I fought off a wave of despair. I was getting nowhere with this girl, absolutely nowhere. Still, I am nothing if not persistent. I continued. "Next comes Post Hoc. Listen to this: Let's not take Bill on our picnic. Every time we take him out with us, it rains."

"I know somebody just like that," she exclaimed. "A girl back home —Eula Becker, her name is. It never fails. Every single time we take her on a picnic—"

"Polly," I said sharply, "it's a fallacy. Eula Becker doesn't cause the rain. She has no connection with the rain. You are guilty of Post Hoc if you blame Eula Becker."

Dicto Simpliciter is Latin for the fallacy of sweeping generalization.

"I'll never do it again," she promised contritely. "Are you mad at me?"

I sighed. "No, Polly, I'm not mad."

"Then tell me some more fallacies."

"All right. Let's try Contradictory Premises."

"Yes, let's," she chirped, blinking her eyes happily.

I frowned, but plunged ahead. "Here's an example of Contradictory Premises: If God can do anything, can He make a stone so heavy that He won't be able to lift it?"

"Of course," she replied promptly.

"But if He can do anything, He can lift the stone," I pointed out.

"Yeah," she said thoughtfully. "Well, then I guess He can't make the stone."

"But He can do anything," I reminded her.

She scratched her pretty, empty head. "I'm all confused," she admitted.

"Of course you are. Because when the premises of an argument contradict each other, there can be no argument. If there is an irresistible force, there can be no immovable object. If there is an immovable object, there can be no irresistible force. Get it?"

"Tell me some more of this keen stuff," she said eagerly.

I consulted my watch. "I think we'd better call it a night. I'll take you home now, and you go over all the things you've learned. We'll have another session tomorrow night."

I deposited her at the girls' dormitory, where she assured me that she had had a perfectly terrif evening, and I went glumly home to my room. Petey lay snoring in his bed, the raccoon coat huddled like a great hairy beast at his feet. For a moment I considered waking him and telling him that he could have his girl back. It seemed clear that my project was doomed to failure. The girl simply had a logic-proof head.

But then I reconsidered. I had wasted one evening; I might as well waste another. Who knew? Maybe somewhere in the extinct crater of her mind a few embers still smoldered. Maybe somehow I could fan them into flame. Admittedly it was not a prospect fraught with hope, but I decided to give it one more try.

Seated under the oak the next evening I said, "Our first fallacy tonight is called Ad Misericordiam."

She quivered with delight.

"Listen closely," I said. "A man applies for a job. When the boss asks him what his qualifications are, he replies that he has a wife and six children at home, the wife is a helpless cripple, the children have nothing to eat, no clothes to wear, no shoes on their feet, there are no beds in the house, no coal in the cellar, and winter is coming."

A tear rolled down each of Polly's pink cheeks. "Oh, this is awful, awful," she sobbed.

"Yes, it's awful," I agreed, "but it's no argument. The man never answered the boss's question about his qualifications. Instead he appealed to the boss's sympathy. He committed the fallacy of Ad Misericordiam. Do you understand?"

"Have you got a handkerchief?" she blubbered.

I handed her a handkerchief and tried to keep from screaming while she wiped her eyes. "Next," I said in a carefully controlled tone, "we will discuss False Analogy. Here is an example: Students should be allowed to look at their textbooks during examinations. After all, surgeons have X-rays to guide them during an operation, lawyers have briefs to guide them during a trial, carpenters have blueprints to guide them when they are building a house. Why, then, shouldn't students be allowed to look at their textbooks during an examination?"

"There now," she said enthusiastically, "is the most marvy idea I've heard in years."

"Polly," I said testily, "the argument is all wrong. Doctors, lawyers, and carpenters aren't taking a test to see how much they have learned, but students are. The situations are altogether different, and you can't make an analogy between them."

"I still think it's a good idea," said Polly.

"Nuts," I muttered. Doggedly I pressed on. "Next we'll try Hypothesis Contrary to Fact."

"Sounds yummy," was Polly's reaction.

"Listen: If Madame Curie had not happened to leave a photographic plate in a drawer with a chunk of pitchblende, the world today would not know about radium."

"True, true," said Polly, nodding her head. "Did you see the movie? Oh, it just knocked me out. That Walter Pidgeon is so dreamy. I mean he fractures me."

"If you can forget Mr. Pidgeon for a moment," I said coldly, "I would like to point out that the statement is a fallacy. Maybe Madame Curie would have discovered radium at some later date. Maybe somebody else would have discovered it. Maybe any number of things would have happened. You can't start with a hypothesis that is not true and then draw any supportable conclusions from it."

"They ought to put Walter Pidgeon in more pictures," said Polly. "I hardly ever see him anymore."

One more chance, I decided. But just one more. There is a limit to what flesh and blood can bear. "The next fallacy is called Poisoning the Well."

"How cute!" she gurgled.

"Two men are having a debate. The first one gets up and says, 'My opponent is a notorious liar. You can't believe a word that he is going to say.' . . . Now, Polly, think. Think hard. What's wrong?"

I watched her closely, as she knit her creamy brow in concentration. Suddenly a glimmer of intelligence—the first I had seen—came into her eyes. "It's not fair," she said with indignation. "It's not a bit fair. What chance has the second man got if the first man calls him a liar before he even begins talking?"

"Right!" I cried exultantly. "One hundred per cent right. It's not fair. The first man has *poisoned the well* before anybody could drink from it. He has hamstrung his opponent before he could even start. . . . Polly, I'm proud of you."

"Pshaw," she murmured, blushing with pleasure.

"You see, my dear, these things are not so hard. All you have to do is concentrate. Think—examine—evaluate. Come now, let's review everything we have learned."

"Fire away," she said with an airy wave of her hand.

Heartened by the knowledge that Polly was not altogether a cretin, I began a long, patient review of all I had told her. Over and over and over again I cited instances, pointed out flaws, kept hammering away without letup. It was like digging a tunnel. At first everything was work, sweat, and darkness. I had no idea when I would reach the light, or even *if* I would. But I persisted. I pounded and clawed and scraped, and finally I was rewarded. I saw a chink of light. And then the chink got bigger and the sun came pouring in and all was bright.

Five grueling nights this took, but it was worth it. I had made a logician out of Polly; I had taught her to think. My job was done. She was worthy of me at last. She was a fit wife for me, a proper hostess for my many mansions, a suitable mother for my well-heeled children.

It must not be thought that I was without love for this girl. Quite the contrary. Just as Pygmalion loved the perfect woman he had fashioned, so I loved mine. I decided to acquaint her with my feelings at our very next meeting. The time had come to change our relationship from academic to romantic.

"Polly," I said when next we sat beneath our oak, "tonight we will not discuss fallacies."

"Aw, gee," she said, disappointed.

"My dear," I said, favoring her with a smile, "we have now spent five evenings together. We have gotten along splendidly. It is clear that we are well matched."

"Hasty Generalization," she repeated. "How can you say that we are well matched on the basis of only five dates?"

I chuckled with amusement. The dear child had learned her lessons well. "My dear," I said, patting her hand in a tolerant manner, "five dates is plenty. After all, you don't have to eat a whole cake to know that it's good."

"False Analogy," said Polly promptly. "I'm not a cake. I'm a girl."

I chuckled with somewhat less amusement. The dear child had learned her lessons perhaps too well. I decided to change tactics. Obviously the best approach was a simple, strong, direct declaration of love. I paused for a moment while my massive brain chose the proper words. Then I began:

"Polly, I love you. You are the whole world to me, and the moon and the stars and the constellations of outer space. Please, my darling, say that you will go steady with me, for if you will not, life will be meaningless. I will languish. I will refuse my meals. I will wander the face of the earth, a shambling, hollow-eyed hulk."

There, I thought, folding my arms, that ought to do it.

"Ad Misericordiam," said Polly.

I ground my teeth. I was not Pygmalion; I was Frankenstein, and my monster had me by the throat. Frantically I fought back the tide of panic surging through me. At all costs I had to keep cool.

"Well, Polly," I said, forcing a smile, "you certainly have learned your fallacies."

"You're darn right," she said with a vigorous nod.

"And who taught them to you, Polly?"

"You did."

"That's right. So you do owe me something, don't you, my dear? If I hadn't come along you never would have learned about fallacies."

"Hypothesis Contrary to Fact," she said instantly.

I dashed perspiration from my brow. "Polly," I croaked, "you mustn't take all these things so literally. I mean this is just classroom stuff. You know that the things you learn in school don't have anything to do with life."

"Dicto Simpliciter," she said, wagging her finger at me playfully.

That did it. I leaped to my feet, bellowing like a bull. "Will you or will you not go steady with me?"

"I will not," she replied.

"Why not?" I demanded.

"Because this afternoon I promised Petey Bellows that I would go steady with him."

I reeled back, overcome with the infamy of it. After he promised, after he made a deal, after he shook my hand! "The rat!" I shrieked, kicking up great chunks of turf. "You can't go with him, Polly. He's a liar. He's a cheat. He's a rat."

"Poisoning the Well," said Polly, "and stop shouting. I think shouting must be a fallacy too."

With an immense effort of will, I modulated my voice. "All right," I said. "You're a logician. Let's look at this thing logically. How could you choose Petey Bellows over me? Look at me—a brilliant student, a tremendous intellectual, a man with an assured future. Look at Petey— a knothead, a jitterbug, a guy who'll never know where his next meal is coming from. Can you give me one logical reason why you should go steady with Petey Bellows?"

"I certainly can," declared Polly. "He's got a raccoon coat."

EXPOSING ILLOGICAL THINKING

All arguments consist of three basic parts:

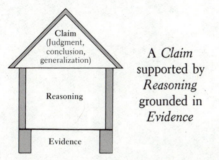

A *Claim* supported by *Reasoning* grounded in *Evidence*

Obviously, if the evidence offered is inadequate, false, or entirely absent, it cannot support valid reasoning. And if the reasoning is fallacious, it cannot support valid conclusions.

Hence the illustration of a house—roof, walls, foundation. Think of a claim as the roof. To stand, it must be supported by strong walls, which in turn must be supported by a firm foundation. Major flaws in either the foundation or in the walls will cause the roof to fall. Similarly, in argument, the *evidence* offered must be *true,* and the *reasoning* based on that evidence must be *sound.*

This book isn't meant to qualify you as a building inspector, but it is meant to qualify you as a knowledgeable argument inspector—and that's *a feat* in itself.

A Blockbuster

During World War II, the term "blockbuster" was used to describe an especially large bomb capable of demolishing an entire city block. The "blockbuster" described in this chapter has no such military application, but it is nonetheless a powerful and important weapon in the reasoning person's battle against illogic and confused thinking.

In evaluating any argument, use the A FEAT acronym as a checklist for assessing the soundness of the argument:

A   Does the argument contain any hidden *Assumptions* that are dubious, questionable, or downright false?

F   Does the argument display one or more of the logical *Fallacies* we have discussed?

E   Does the argument employ *Empty abstractions?*

A   Are there potential *Alternative explanations* for the cause → effect relationship alleged?

T   Is the *Truth* of the evidence questionable?

If your answer to any of these questions is "Yes"—BLAMO. The blockbuster just went off, the roof just caved in, the claim supported by the argument just disintegrated.

To illustrate:

Argument: "The poem 'Richard Cory' isn't realistic. Cory had good looks, wealth, and respect, so there was no reason for his suicide."

Assumption: "People who are handsome, wealthy, and respected are always happy."

Discrediting: Cite exceptions: friends of your parents, movie stars, rock musicians, authors, and others who have possessed good looks, wealth, and respect yet have committed or attempted suicide.

Argument: "The Equal Rights movement threatens the very core of social stability. If women are to be granted equal rights with men, then why not children with adults, the insane with the sane, and criminals with law-abiding citizens. The result would be total anarchy."

Fallacy: Slippery slope.

Discrediting: Explain the nature of the specific fallacy involved.

Argument: "We must rededicate ourselves to decency and integrity."

Empty Abstractions: "dedicate," "decency," "integrity"

Discrediting: Without examples to clarify and specify what the speaker or writer has in mind, abstractions are mere sound and fury, signifying nothing. (Note also the hidden assumption implied by the term *"re*dedicate.")

Argument: "Imprisonment is at least partially effective as a means of reformation because 20 to 40 percent of offenders imprisoned never return to prison after being released."

Alternative Explanations: (1) Some, most, or all of this 20 to 40 percent continued to commit crimes but were not arrested, convicted, and imprisoned. (2) This 20 to 40 percent reformed *in spite of* rather than *because of* imprisonment. Without imprisonment, a larger percentage might have reformed.

Discrediting: No cause→effect conclusion is warranted when alternative explanations exist.

Argument: "Education without God produces a nation without freedom."

Truth: The burden of supplying evidence and proving the contention always rests on the person making the argument. Mere allegation in the absence of sufficient evidence and sound reasoning is meaningless.

Discrediting: "Prove it."

APPLICATIONS: A BLOCKBUSTER

Do *A FEAT* on each of the following arguments. For each argument, identify any:

*A*ssumptions
*F*allacies

*E*mpty abstractions
*A*lternative explanations
*T*ruth doubtfulness

1. To require the president to consult with Congress before acting on matters of national security is absurd. Why, if Christopher Columbus had been required to take a vote among his crew every time he wanted to do something, he would never have discovered America.

2. "I don't permit questions in class because if one student asks questions then all the students should be able to ask questions, and then there wouldn't be any time for my lectures."

   college professor

3. "We've just sent to Congress proposed new amendments that would put real teeth into the Fair Housing Law."

   Vice-President George H. W. Bush

4. As a friend of Mary's, you've just *got* to tell her about seeing John kissing that strange woman. After all, honesty is the best policy.

5. "It's obvious that prosperity doesn't decrease crime, just as it's obvious that deprivation and want don't necessarily increase crime. It's my recollection that crime rates were at their lowest during the depression of the Thirties, when great numbers of people were destitute. Today's criminals, for the most part, are not desperate people seeking bread for their families. Crime is the way they've chosen to live."

   Ronald Reagan

6. "If my mother was a beautiful actress, known and respected around the world for 50 years for her talent, and I was a fat, sanctimonious Bible thumper, I would probably write a nasty book about her too."

   Reader comment about B. D. Hymon's biography of her mother,
   Bette Davis

7. "Sex education without morals is like breakfast without orange juice."

   Evangelist David Noebel

8. "It is possible to stop most drug addiction in the United States

within a very short time. Simply make all drugs available and sell them at cost."

Gore Vidal

9. "As long as we persist in thinking that only government can solve problems of poverty and social disintegration, the prospect of any breakthroughs in those areas will remain bleak."

Father Bruce Ritter

10. "Fish or cut bait."

popular saying

11. "Fleischmann's gin is clean . . . clean . . . clean."

advertisement

12. "If you're not part of the solution, you're part of the problem."

popular saying

13. "The goal of our research project is to uncover the precipitating event in the subjects' childhood which caused them to develop agoraphobia."

grant proposal

14. "The great powers must still determine the kind of role they are to play in the Middle East—whether they are to revert to power politics or to undertake to advance and enforce a compromise peace through the United Nations."

Senator J. W. Fulbright

15. Some say that since our nation benefits from well-educated university graduates, such education should be provided at state cost. This is absurd. After all, the country also benefits from a well-fed, well-housed, and healthy population. But this does not mean that the government should provide everybody with free food, housing, and health care.

16. "Cola drinkers were asked to compare glasses of Coke with Pepsi. The Coke was in a glass marked Q, the Pepsi in a glass marked M. The majority of those tested said they preferred the taste of Pepsi."

advertisement

17. "When the going gets tough, the tough get going."

    popular saying

18. I don't see why I have to be home by eleven when lots of my girlfriends get to stay out as late as they want.

19. How can you say you don't believe in miracles? The sunrise that occurs every day is a miracle.

20. I really can't take your arguments very seriously, son. After all, what does a sixteen-year-old know about life?

21. No one objects when a physician looks up a difficult case in a medical text. Why, then, shouldn't students taking a difficult exam be permitted to use *their* textbook?

22. "A top Agriculture Department official said Friday that retail food prices are not too high, because if they were, the housewife would back out of the marketplace and the cost would go down."

    news report, AP

23. "The most dramatic evidence of the relationship between education practices and civil disorder lies in the high incidence of riot participation by ghetto youth who have not completed high school. Our survey of the riot cities found that the typical riot participant was a high school dropout."

    Report of the National Advisory Commission on Civil Disorder

24. "It is high time those who distort the perspective of young minds, who advocate the overthrow of our system of government, who corrupt and pervert the education process, be purged from our educational institutions . . . .

    "There is something dreadfully wrong with college governing boards and administrators which allow faculties . . . to become overloaded with fuzzy-minded, phony liberals whose heros are Che Guevara, Fidel Castro, Ho Chi Minh, and Mao Tse-tung."

    Senator Robert C. Byrd

25. "To be sure, some drugs are more dangerous than others. It is easier to kill oneself with heroin than with aspirin. But it is also easier to kill oneself by jumping off a high building than a low one. . . .

"Therefore, it is absurd to deprive an adult of a drug (or of anything else) because he might use it to kill himself."

Thomas S. Szasz, M.D.

26. The welfare program is a big ripoff of the working American. I know a guy who runs a numbers racket and drives a brand new Cadillac, and every week he goes downtown to collect his welfare check.

27. "One of the dreams that lulls us into this hopeful make-believe is the theory of the so-called atomic standoff. This is the argument that, when both we and the Communists have plenty of atomic weapons, neither of us will use them. To gamble on such a miracle is like betting that two men armed with loaded pistols will merely wrestle until one of them is thrown to the ground and kicked to death."

Senator Stuart Symington

28. "I too, am against [Michigan's] seat belt law. In fact, it infuriates me! Does the government own me? It is my life to do with what I wish.

"Driving in an unfamiliar city late at night in heavy rain, my car suddenly dropped off 100 feet into 50 feet of water. There was a drawbridge opened to allow a freighter to pass through. There were no lights, no bells, no whistles, no gates—nothing to warn me. The force of the water blew my car's canvas top off and I rose, unconscious, to the surface. A sailor who was waiting to return to his freighter dove in to rescue me. Had I been wearing a seat belt, I wouldn't be alive today.

"In another incident reported in the *Free Press* recently, a heroic man rushed to rescue two women in a burning car but could not because they were wearing seat belts."

letter to the editor

29. "Insensitive television coverage of the plight of the TWA Flight 847 hostages may have endangered them and prolonged their captivity, according to some top U.S. officials involved in negotiations for their release.

"Other analysts, outside the administration, said that President Reagan's threats of reprisals just as the hostages were about to be released lengthened their ordeal.

"As for TV's role, 'Before the cameras arrived, terrorists beat and murdered an American sailor,' noted Michael Robinson, director of the Media Analysis Project at George Washington University. 'After the cameras arrived, no one was hurt,' Robinson said. 'TV, once again, made it more difficult for the hijackers to brutalize and murder their captives.'"

news feature

30. The essence of a democracy is that the government should follow the will of the majority. So if a majority of U.S. citizens want prayer in the public schools, that's what we should have.

31. People will gamble anyway, so why not legalize gambling in this state?

32. We should encourage a return to arranged marriages, since marriages based on romantic love haven't been very successful.

33. "The separation of religion and politics ended when the state started trying to redefine right and wrong in pornography, abortion, race, economics and the relation of the sexes."

Joseph Sobron, Boston Globe

34. "We must judge this issue by what the Bible says, not by what we think it says or by what some scholar or theologian thinks it says."

radio preacher

35. America cannot compete with Japanese imports because the Japanese pay their workers much lower wages.

36. "Ever wonder why kids instinctively go for soft drinks in bottles?"

Glass Container Manufacturers Institute

37. Physical education should be required because physical activity is healthful.

38. "If I quit [my book-banning efforts] with 'Deenie' it would be the same if my house were on fire and I only put the fire out in one corner."

Theresa Wilson, Concerned Citizens of Gwinnett

39. "Anybody who is intelligent will be polygynous. You can't go on eating Italian food forever. Once in a while you want to try a Chinese restaurant. Marriage is a lifelong bondage."

Guru Shree Rajnees

40. The idea of labeling or rating records containing explicit sexual lyrics is "the equivalent of treating dandruff by decapitation."

rock singer Frank Zappa

REASONING AND RHETORIC

Reasoning can take place in our minds, but the moment we decide to share that reasoning, whether in speech or in writing, we enter the realm of rhetoric. Thinking may be solitary; rhetoric is always social.

In this final chapter, we take a brief look at some of the social conventions that come into play when the thinker turns writer.

1

Persona

When another person reads what you have written, he or she constructs —usually quite unconsciously—a mental image of you, the writer.

This mental image is called the writer's *persona*. The *persona* of the writer is not the writer as he or she really is. After all, how could a complete stranger reading your work know you for what you really are? Rather, your *persona* is the image or impression of you that the reader gets from such things as your tone, your apparent values, your fair-mindedness (or lack of same), your knowledgeability about your subject, and your writing style.

Unfair? Perhaps. But inevitable nonetheless. And true of many others besides writers. Actors, for example, worry about getting "typecast." If they play too many roles as a murderous psychopath (Tony Perkins), a macho male (Clint Eastwood), or a brainless sex object (Bo Derek), the viewing public may refuse to accept them in substantially different roles. *Persona* has triumphed over person; what they appear to be has become more real to others than what they are.

Robert Young, who played the role of Dr. Welby in the television series "Marcus Welby, M.D.," reports that he was deluged with mail asking for his professional medical opinion about the correspondents' physical illnesses. There is a documented case in which a cowboy, watching a melodramatic play, stood up from the audience and shot the man playing the role of the villain. To the confused cowboy, the actor's *persona*—what he appeared to be—had become reality. And, of course, when we speak of an advertising agency "packaging" a candidate and when we complain about how campaign strategists shape a politician's image, we are also speaking of the candidate's *persona*.

What's all this have to do with writing? Just this: *Persona* is real.

To the reader, the *persona* you project is you. If the way you deal with your subject strikes the reader as responsible, thoughtful, balanced, and well-informed, these positive qualities will be ascribed to you, the author. And because we are inclined to heed the views of people we respect, your credibility will be enhanced and your argument will carry extra weight.

2

Rhetorical Stance

Wayne C. Booth defines *rhetorical stance* as "A proper balance between the three elements at work in any communicative effort: the available arguments on the subject, the interests and peculiarities of the audience, and the voice—the implied character of the speaker [or writer]."

For effective persuasive writing, sound reasoning is not sufficient. You must also consider the nature of your audience: their interests and peculiarities; their presumed values, knowledgeability, and maturity; their potential sympathy, neutrality, skepticism, or hostility toward the thesis you are advocating.

Psychologist Carl Rogers has observed that people—all people—are easily threatened creatures. Beliefs and viewpoints different from those we already hold threaten our sense of identity and integrity, causing us to reject them. The more important the values and attitudes being challenged, the greater the reader's resistance to accepting them.

Thus, to reason *persuasively*, you must not only reason well but also minimize the sense of threat your ideas may arouse in your audience. To do so, ask yourself how you can create "bridges" between yourself and your audience by emphasizing shared values, common goals, mutual needs.

The purpose of argumentative writing is to convince or persuade, to make the reader agree with your opinion, or take some action, or both. The surest way *not* to achieve this purpose is to write entirely from your own personal perspective without considering your audience.

The student–author of the letter reprinted below wanted to persuade the editor of his hometown newspaper to include more coverage of local sports events. Here's what he wrote:

Mrs. Betty Noteware, Editor
Manistee NEWS ADVOCATE
Manistee, Michigan

Dear Mrs. Noteware:

The coverage of county sports events in your paper is lousy. During
recent years the county's sports programs have received very little or
even NO coverage at all. This is sickening. Oh, there's nothing very
much wrong with the sports writer except he could not even write a
decent obituary, let alone an entire sports page.

Well over half the papers which the Manistee NEWS ADVOCATE
sells are purchased by people that live in the rural area surrounding
Manistee, and whose children attend rural schools. If all the people who
have an interest in sports at the county level would cancel their
subscription to the NEWS ADVOCATE, it would tickle me to no end.

Sincerely yours,

Stanley Finan
Concerned Manistee County
Citizen

The letter is virtually guaranteed to evoke anger instead of action.
The *persona* of the writer is alienating instead of engaging. He appears
immature, judgmental, hostile, vindictive, and sarcastic—scarcely the
sort of person whose views we would be inclined to consider.

If your purpose is argumentative, put yourself in the place of your
audience. What considerations are most likely to sway them? What
objections are they likely to raise? What shared values can you emphasize to win a sympathetic hearing? Note how this rewritten version of
the letter to the editor differs from the original:

Mrs. Betty Noteware, Editor
Manistee NEWS ADVOCATE
Manistee, Michigan

Dear Mrs. Noteware:

As a native of Manistee, I have been a long-time subscriber to your
newspaper. The thoughtfulness of your editorials and your in-depth
analysis of national events have always impressed me as outstanding
qualities of the NEWS ADVOCATE.

In one particular area, however, I feel there is room for improvement. Even though most of the subscribers to the NEWS ADVOCATE live in the greater Manistee area and are thus closely identified with the local scene, the coverage of county sports is often spotty and thin. I cannot help believing that fuller coverage of local and regional sports would enhance the NEWS ADVOCATE's appeal and might well win your paper new subscribers. Such additional coverage would also demonstrate your concern for the community that supports the NEWS ADVOCATE and your support for the sports events that interest so many members of the community.

I hope you will consider my comments in the spirit in which they are offered. Increased coverage of the local sports scene would make an already fine newspaper finer.

Sincerely yours,

Stanley Finan

One of the major differences between the two versions of the letter is the vast difference in tone. The tone of the original is sarcastic, abrasive, and hostile; the tone of the revision is mild and reasonable. "Tone" refers to the author's attitude toward his subject or audience, as communicated through his style of writing. The tone of a composition may be formal, informal, or intimate; it may be solemn, serious, humorous, ironic, indignant, sarcastic, or condescending. Sentence structure, diction, choice of examples, and nature of presentation all help to establish tone.

No one tone is intrinsically superior to any other tone. But the tone you adopt should be appropriate to your subject, your audience, and your purpose.

3

The Internalized Reader

To write well, we need to become a little schizoid. We need to construct an adult equivalent to the fantasy playmate children sometimes create. Let's give this imaginary creature a fancy name: the "Internalized Reader."

What does the Internalized Reader (I.R.) do? Mainly, he or she asks doubting questions, challenges our generalizations, and demands more evidence.

"Who says?" I.R. questions. "Aren't you overstating a bit there?" I.R. challenges. "How about a couple of examples to make that point clear," I.R. demands.

Listen. And obey. I. R. is your friend. I. R. is on your side. I. R. wants to save you from mistakes that will confuse, alienate, or anger real readers in the real world.

Effective writing is not a monologue but a dialogue—an interaction between two people, the writer and the reader. In conversation, this is obvious. The person we're speaking with nods, shakes his or her head, frowns, smiles, leans forward or away, questions, objects, and requests clarification—dialogue.

When people read an essay or report we've written, they do precisely the same thing, only mentally rather than out loud. They mentally frown in disagreement, shake their heads in puzzlement, wish for a clarifying example, and so forth. The dialogue is taking place, just as in conversation, but it's taking place at two separate points in time rather than at a single point in time as in conversation.

In order to communicate clearly and persuasively, we need to bring our future readers into our minds as we write, watching for frowns and head shakes, listening for requests for clarification. In short, we need to answer the future readers' objections and ease their confusion as we write. But we can't do that unless we have a reader inside our brains to converse with as we write. Hence the writer's best friend: the Internalized Reader.

HIGHLIGHTS

* Thinking may be solitary; rhetoric is always social.
* To the reader, the *persona* you project is you.
* To reason persuasively, you must not only reason well but also minimize the sense of threat your ideas may arouse in your audience.
* The tone you adopt should be appropriate to your subject, your audience, and your purpose.
* Effective writing is not a monologue but a dialogue—an interaction between two people, the writer and the reader.

APPLICATIONS: REASONING AND RHETORIC

The ultimate purpose of argumentative writing is persuasion. The ultimate effect of illogic, inaccuracy, or abrasiveness in such writing is to fail at persuasion. When you write, you are the teacher and the reader is your student. Illogical argument and factual inaccuracy break the chain of trust that sustains this relationship.

Like the little boy who cries "Wolf!" in the fable, the writer who appears unreasonable or ill informed loses credibility with the reader. And without credibility a teacher cannot instruct, nor a writer convince.

The readings that follow exemplify this principle. In each case, or so it seems to me, the "chain of trust" binding reader and writer snaps. Persuasion fails.

As you read these arguments, see whether the chain of trust breaks for you also. If it does, try to determine why. For each selection:

Find and underline statements that you believe to be *factually* inaccurate.

Find and underline instances where the writer makes a statement involving a questionable or false hidden generalization.

Find and label specific logical fallacies discussed in this text.

Find and label examples of unconcretized abstractions.

Indicate what you believe to be the most glaring or most pervasive reasoning error.

Briefly describe each author's *persona*. In other words, what impressions of the author's character and personality are communicated by the way the author deals with his or her subject?

1. THE IMPORTANCE OF DISCIPLINE

"Go to bed."

"No."

Thwak!

Discipline is a "touchy" subject. Children do get out of hand these days; they get away with murder. Should they be disciplined? Should the punishment be physical?

A lot of people, especially those with an interest in psychology, are of the new school that kids should not be punished for their wrong doings. Hitting a kid is unforgivable, the cardinal sin. Those nuts want you to talk it over with the wretched runt. They think you should encourage the brat to give you the reasons for his/her behavior, find out if the kid thinks what he/she did was wrong, and why.

My parents, on the other hand, are of the old school. If a kid's moving down the wrong road to life, give it not a push, but a good, swift kick in the right direction. I may be spoiled, but I certainly was not spared the rod. I feel that a good old-fashioned spanking is a lot more effective at teaching right and wrong than a silly question like, "Did you gain personal satisfaction from pulling sister's hair?" What if the kid says, "Yes, I like pulling sister's hair. I feel much better when I pull sister's hair."

Do children learn what is right and wrong from "Don't do that, it's not nice"? I don't think so. However, if you smack the misbehaving little rug rat, that is a very good incentive not to do it again, right or wrong. If it feels good, do it. If it hurts, don't. It's not a difficult concept to understand, even for a kid.

What if the terrible two-year-old is sticking something into an electrical outlet, or reaching out to touch a hot iron? Are you going to reason with little Robert on the causes and effects of death and/or serious injury and its relationship with pain? I wouldn't waste valuable time. I would knock little Robert clear to the other side of the room and say, "Little Robert, if you ever go near that again, Mommy's going to beat you senseless." Take my word for it. This way has immediate and lasting results.

When I say "beat," I do not mean "abuse." The "Board of Education" need only be strong enough to persuade. The kid must be taught that whatever he/she is doing, not doing it feels much better.

Kids are not dumb, only ignorant. They are ignorant of the fact that they will be scalded by the boiling liquid in the pan if they pull it off the stove. However, they are not ignorant of the fact that if you hit them for even attempting such a thing, it would not be a good idea to try it again.

Theodore Roosevelt once said, "Speak softly, but carry a big stick." Just remember, when it comes to disciplining kids, the stick should be forcefully applied.

2. Sin, Sex, TV
JAMES J. KILPATRICK

The dictionary defines "crusade" as a remedial enterprise undertaken with zeal. People who act with zeal perforce are zealots, and zealots are first cousins of fanatics, and all this is why the Rev. Donald Wildmon and his followers give me the blue willies.

The Rev. Mr. Wildmon, as you may have read, is engaged in a crusade against sex and sin on television. He rounded up 4,000 like-minded volunteers across the country, and for three months these observers solemnly annotated every shot, every kiss, every damn or hell and every jiggle on the tube. When they were done, the reverend ran the results through a computer. Then he put some heavy pressure on the sponsors of the programs deemed most objectionable.

The Procter & Gamble people, who spend almost $500 million a year on TV advertising, quickly got the point. Said board chairman Owen Butler to the networks: "I can assure you that we are listening very carefully to what they say." Mr. Butler thought the reverend's National Federation for Decency was expressing "some very important and broadly held views about gratuitous sex, violence and profanity."

For a while there was talk of a boycott against the products of the offending sponsors, but that talk has subsided. The writers and producers of such bummers as "The Dukes of Hazzard" have stopped muttering about censorship and artistic freedom. For the time being the controversy has blown over, but my blue willies remain. Two of the best rules for happy human relations are "Live and let live," and "Mind your own durned business." Why don't we observe them?

These issues ought to be decided in the marketplace. That is one of the things a free society is all about. Implicit in the intolerance of the Wildmon crusaders is the prospect that if they don't like a particular program, nobody else should be able to see it either. That is zealotry in action, and it is an ugly business.

The Mississippi reverend says his crusade is supported by five million families in all 50 states. Maybe yes, maybe no. That leaves roughly 54 million other families unaccounted for. Ninety-eight percent of all these families have television sets, and there is this interesting characteristic about those TV sets. Every one of them has a little switch that is lettered in this fashion: "On" and "Off."

Nothing in this world—no law, no regulation, no economic pressure, nothing at all—compels the reverend and his friends to watch "Dallas" or the "Dukes" or "Flamingo Road." His 4,000 observers and the members of his five million families are freeborn American citizens. It is a reasonable presumption that every one of them is capable of manipulating the little switch. All they have to do in order to avoid offense is to turn the switch to "Off."

Commercial television, let us remember, is just that—a commercial enterprise. The folks at Proctor & Gamble are not sponsoring particular programs out of altruistic motives. They are not concerned with promoting art, but with selling soap. Once a program fails to attract sufficient viewers to sell sufficient soap, the program will be dropped. This is how the marketplace works.

But the manipulation of the little switch, it seems to me, ought to be by individual decision and not by mass persuasion. Live and let live! It is not essential to a contented and productive existence that we watch television by day and by night. There are books to be read, and letters to be written, and pickles to be pickled, and a thousand other enterprises and amusements to pass the time. What do Mr. Wildmon's five million families do when they are being offended by "Three's Company"? Maybe they could just sit around the kitchen table and talk. It's a wholesome thought.

One of these days, these essentially trivial exercises in censorship will be trampled underfoot by technology. Before this century ends, all of us will have access to TV entertainment across the whole spectrum from good works to go-go girls. Come the millennium, these crusaders will be out of work—and not a day too soon.

3. Nader: Who Asked Him to Mind Our Business?

Recently the news media have observed the 20th anniversary of the publication of Ralph Nader's famous book, "Unsafe at Any Speed." I am writing to comment on the occasion.

I consider Mr. Nader a tyrant who thinks that because some things (i.e., sleek automobiles) are offensive to him, everybody else should share his view. If another, equally puritanical individual wanted to outlaw Playboy magazine, birth control etc., I doubt many liberals would consider him or her a hero. Strangely, they do not similarly reject Nader.

Take the air bag issue. If somebody wants an air bag for his or her own car, fine. But where is the justice when 100 million motorists are forced to have air bags, whether they like it or not, to satisfy the emotional needs of Nader and his followers? Even if a large percentage of people were to choose air bags, demanding that they be mandatory is like saying that if 90 percent of the people choose automatic transmissions, manual transmissions should be illegal.

Likewise, I fail to see the justice of forcing millions of Americans to accept cars whose comfort, performance, even safety are compromised by increasingly stringent fuel economy regulations, again, to satisfy the needs of people like Nader.

We all have our personal hangups, to varying degrees. What makes Nader and his followers different is that they seek public solutions for their private furies. It is time for all of us who value freedom of choice to demand that so-called consumer activists, who cannot leave other people alone, seek solutions for their private hangups where such problems ought to be solved—on a psychiatrist's couch.

As for idealistic college students seeking to enter the consumer activism arena, it is high time we teach our youth that there are times, honestly, when minding one's own business is the better part of good citizenship.

Alexander R. Kovnat
Oak Park*

*Letter to the Detroit *Free Press,* Dec. 16, 1985, p. 8-A. Reprinted by permission of the Detroit *Free Press.*

4.

Bravo to the [Detroit] *Free Press* for the courageous Dec. 2 [1985] editorial, "Execution: It's a barbaric practice no civilized state should adopt." Michigan citizens must be made aware of all the facts about the death penalty and its application. Somehow L. Brooks Patterson [leader of drive advocating Michigan's adoption of the death penalty] never gets around to them.

Let the purveyors of hysteria and the proponents of legalized murder beware. We have not yet begun to fight and in due course, we will expose those who stump for a return to barbarism for what they truly are: political opportunists.

The people of this great state are not as gullible as Patterson might think. They will respond to the abundance of material about state-sanctioned killing as any right-thinking people would and they will vote down this hideous proposal.

Yes, the battle is on, and may the forces of reason prevail over demogoguery.

> *Patrick Thompson*
> Co-ordinator
> Michigan Coalition Against the Death Penalty
> Lansing*

5.

The 55 m.p.h. speed limit was put into effect as a result of a nationwide fuel shortage caused by escalating prices of crude oil. At the time, the limit was referred to as a "temporary measure," implying that once the fuel crisis eased, the limit would return to the original 70 m.p.h. Eleven years later, with the worldwide oil glut and fuel prices stabilized, the 55 m.p.h. limit remains in effect.

One of President Reagan's campaign platforms in the '80 election called for the abolishment of the 55 m.p.h. limit. Yet, no action has been taken, well into the president's second term. Politicians and law enforcement officials continue to support the limit, stating over and over that it "saves gas and lives," while ignoring the fact that today's cars are much safer and more fuel efficient than 11 years ago, accounting for

*Detroit *Free Press*, December 14, 1985. Reprinted by permission of the Detroit *Free Press*.

many of the lowered statistics. Also ignored is that several states, including Michigan, have mandatory seat belt laws, lowering fatalities even further.

As a full-time college student who must hold down an afternoon shift job in order to pay for my schooling, I often have to drive directly from school to work, a distance of some forty miles. For myself, driving 60 to 65 m.p.h. means the difference between getting to work on time or being late, which my employer does not take too kindly to.

When Prohibition was first instituted in 1920, it was felt to be a necessary law. Later, when the government realized that it was no longer applicable, the law was repealed. I feel the same time has come for the 55 m.p.h. speed limit.

Steven J. Ramberger
St. Clair Shores*

*Detroit *Free Press*, October 7, 1985, p. 8-A. Reprinted by permission of the Detroit *Free Press*.

NOTES

1. James G. Martin, *The Tolerant Personality* (Detroit: Wayne State University Press), p. 64.
2. Clyde Kluckhohn, *Mirror for Man* (New York: McGraw-Hill, 1949), p. 160.
3. Matt Mahoney, A. Sutton, and C. Panati, *Digital Communications* (New York: R.C.A. Institute for Professional Development, 1968).
4. From Ernest Hemingway, *A Farewell to Arms* (New York: Scribner's, 1957), pp. 184–185.
5. J. Edgar Hoover, *Vital Speeches of the Day* (October 1, 1957).
6. Jenkin Lloyd Jones, "Almost Anything Goes," *The Tulsa Tribune* (August 22, 1959).
7. Mike Duffy, "The Hell of Sexual Harassment," The Detroit *Free Press* (May 18, 1980), Section H, p. 1.
8. From *Strictly Personal* by Sidney J. Harris © by and permission of News America Syndicate.
9. Sir James Jeans, *The Stars in Their Courses.* Copyrighted by and reprinted by permission of Cambridge University Press.

GLOSSARY OF FALLACIES*

Ad hominem. Also called the *genetic fallacy*. Literally argument "against the man," the *ad hominem* fallacy substitutes a personal attack for substantive argument. See *name calling; tu quoque.*

Ad ignorantiam. Literally, an appeal "to ignorance." The fallacy of claiming something is true because it cannot be disproved or that something is untrue because it cannot be proved. The burden of proving a generalization always rests on the person making the assertion. Argument *ad ignorantiam* says, in effect, "Because you can't prove I'm wrong, I'm right."

Ad populum. Literally, appeal "to the people." The fallacy of seeking approval by appealing to the prejudices, preconceptions, and popular beliefs of the masses.

*A-major syllogism. A syllogism with an affirmative (A) major premise.

Appeal to authority. The fallacy of presuming that the views of a high-status individual are true simply because of that person's high repute. To carry weight, the opinions of an expert must relate to the field he or she is knowledgeable about.

Appeal to fear. The fallacy of coercing agreement by implying or alleging that one's opponent will be harmed unless he or she agrees with a proposition.

Appeal to pity. The fallacy of obscuring an issue by arousing emotions of sympathy, compassion, and guilt.

Argumentative analogy. See *false analogy.*

Bandwagon. The fallacy of supporting a conclusion by claiming its acceptance by most other people or a large number of them.

Begging the question. The fallacy of "supporting" a generalization,

---

*All *new* technical terms used in explaining specific fallacies are defined in separate entries marked with asterisks.

judgment, or conclusion by repeating it in different words. For example:

"The Chinese can't be trusted."
"Why not?"
"Because they're devious."

Common practice. The fallacy of arguing that an action is acceptable because it is widely practiced by others.

Distortion. The fallacy of misrepresenting the truth and then drawing a conclusion as though that misrepresentation were true. See *straw man* and *unrepresentative sample*.

Double exclusion. See *double negation*.

Double negation. In syllogistic reasoning, the fallacy of reaching a conclusion based on two negative premises. For example:

No computer lasts forever.
People are not computers.
Therefore? (No additional generalization or conclusion can be inferred.)

*Double particular. In syllogistic reasoning, the fallacy of reaching a conclusion without a universal premise. For example:

Some dogs have tails.
Some cats have tails.
Therefore? (No additional generalization or conclusion can be inferred.)

Either–or. Also called *false dilemma*. The fallacy of reducing a number of possible alternatives, attitudes, or positions to two polar opposites. See also *oversimplification*.

Equivocation. The use of the same word in two different senses in an argument. The fallacy of equivocation involves shifting the meaning of a key term without acknowledging that shift and then reverting to the original sense of the term in the conclusion.

False analogy. Also called *argumentative analogy*. The fallacy of comparing two dissimilar subjects or situations as though they were similar in some relevant respect.

False dilemma. See *either–or*.

Genetic fallacy. See *ad hominem*.

Hasty conclusion. Also called *hasty generalization*. The fallacy of reaching a conclusion or making a generalization based on insufficient evidence.

*Major class. In syllogistic reasoning, the class that appears in the predicate of the conclusion.

*Major premise. In an A-major syllogism, that premise that mentions the largest of the three classes of the syllogism. In an N-major syllogism, that premise that states a universal negative proposition.

*Middle term. In syllogistic reasoning, the term (or class) that appears in both premises.

*Minor class. In syllogistic reasoning, the class that appears in both premises.

*Minor premise. In syllogistic reasoning, the premise other than the major premise. Also, the premise that contains the subject-term of the conclusion.

*Misplaced exclusion. In an A-major syllogism, the fallacy of reaching a conclusion when the minor premise places the third class outside the minor class. For example:

All frame houses are flammable.
My house is not a frame house.
Therefore my house is not flammable. (invalid conclusion)

*Misplaced inclusion. In an A-major syllogism, the fallacy of reaching a conclusion when the minor premise places the third class inside the major class. For example:

All drunkards are drinkers.
John Smith is a drinker.
Therefore John Smith is a drunkard. (invalid conclusion)

Name calling. The fallacy of attempting to discredit persons or propositions by attaching "bad" names to them. Like *ad hominem,* name calling substitutes ridicule or vilification for substantive argument.

*N-major syllogism. A syllogism with a negative (N) major premise.

*Non sequitur. Meaning "it does not follow," the fallacy of *non sequitur* occurs when a conclusion or generalization "does not follow" from the evidence cited. Hence, *non sequitur* involves supporting a conclusion with an irrelevant reason. For example, during the Vietnam conflict, both the Johnson and Nixon administrations answered charges that the war was morally wrong by countering that such talk only encouraged the enemy and prolonged the fighting. Even if the countercharge was true, it was *irrelevant* to the issue of the war's morality.

Overgeneralization. The fallacy of generalizing about an entire class of people or things on the basis of observing only one or a few.

Oversimplification. Both a cause of fallacious logic and a fallacy in itself, oversimplification refers to any argument in which the complexity of issues and causal relationships is obscured or denied. Fallacies displaying oversimplification include *either–or, false analogy, hasty generalization, sweeping generalization,* and *post hoc.*

Popular passions. See *ad populum.*

Post hoc ergo propter hoc. Literally "after this, therefore because of this." The fallacy of alleging a causal relationship solely on the basis of a chronological relationship.

Red herring. In argument, the fallacy of raising an irrelevant issue to divert attention from the primary issue.

Slippery slope. The fallacy of claiming an action should be avoided because taking it will inevitably lead to other, less desirable actions.

*Straw man. The fallacy of distorting the argument or position of an opponent and then attacking that distorted version. For example, during the 1980 Republican convention, some Democrats alleged that Ronald Reagan was prepared to offer Gerald Ford a "co-presidency" if he would agree to become Reagan's running mate. Having thus distorted Reagan's position, they proceeded to attack a "co-presidency" as absurd, indicating Reagan's desperation and poor judgment.

Sweeping generalization. The fallacy of applying a general principle to a specific case, as though the principle were a rule.

*Syllogism. A structured form of deductive reasoning consisting of a major premise, a minor premise, and a conclusion, involving three classes or terms. The classic illustration of a valid syllogism is:

(middle term)
  (minor class)   (major class)
    All men are mortal.   (major premise)
               (middle term)
(third class) (minor class)
    Socrates is a man.   (minor premise)
("therefore")
  (third class) (major class)
    Socrates is mortal.   (conclusion)

Tu quoque. Literally "You [do it] too" or "You're another," *tu quoque* is the fallacy of justifying an action or position by accusing one's opponent of doing the same thing or something equally reprehensible.

*Undistributed middle. In syllogistic reasoning, the fallacy of drawing a conclusion when the middle term is not universalized (distributed) at least once. For example:

All criminals think it's okay to break the law.
John Smith thinks it's okay to break the law.
Therefore John Smith is a criminal. (invalid conclusion)

Just because two individuals or groups share one characteristic (in this case, the view that it's okay to break the law), it does not follow that they inevitably share other characteristics (in this case, criminal behavior).

Unrepresentative sample. The fallacy of generalizing from a sample population that is not representative of the population as a whole. For example, the advertisement "Ninety percent of doctors surveyed recommended Product X," suggests that 90 percent of all doctors would recommend Product X. But it's quite possible that the company placing the advertisement surveyed only doctors already known to favor Product X, with one exception thrown in for credibility. Unless the sample used as the basis for statistical or other generalizations is known to be fair, unbiased, random, and sufficiently large to be representative of the whole, the generalizations should be viewed with skepticism.

*Validity. A term used in evaluating deductive arguments. Strictly speaking, a deductive argument is said to be *valid* when its conclusion follows logically and necessarily from its premises. For the conclusion of a valid argument to be true, the premises must be true.

INDEX

ABOUT THE AUTHOR

RAY KYTLE is former Director of Composition and current Coordinator of Creative Writing at Central Michigan University. In addition to professional articles, Kytle has authored numerous college texts in the areas of rhetoric, logic, language, and literary criticism. Professor Kytle has also published several novels, the most recent of which was adapted for television.